Praise for *Radical Healership* from Practicing Healers

"Laura Northrup skillfully breaks down how to embark on and build an ethical and *successful* healing arts practice—one committed to both individual and collective healing. This book covers everything from connecting to your purpose and committing to your own healing to the ins and outs of sharing your work publicly and working to dismantle oppressive lenses in ourselves and in our work with others. A fulfilling, ethical, financially viable practice committed to dismantling systemic oppression and supporting people in their healing is possible. If you're looking for an anti-oppressive, anti-capitalist, spiritually led book to help you start or build your healing arts practice, start right here."

—JENNIFER PATTERSON, healing arts practitioner, author of
The Power of Breathwork, and editor of the anthology *Queering
Sexual Violence*

"In this brave and compelling book, Laura Northrup brings humanity to the experience of being a healer. She approaches how to be authentic healers in a capitalist world like a pugilist entering the ring—both feet on the ground with total pragmatic dedication to the fight. Written more like a moving letter from a close friend than a know-it-all tutorial, this book's disarming humor and relatable stories take down the Titan of self-doubt like a silver bullet. This is a must-read for all health professionals, nurses, caregivers, artists, lovers, mystics—and anyone looking to find their footing in this world."

—ALESE OSBORN, tarot reader, Oracular artist, and host of
the podcast *Neon Cauldron*

"A poignant and deep psychological and sociological analysis of why healers don't succeed, as well as a guide to doing the inner work so that they can. This is the book I wish I had as a new practitioner."

—CHASE DESSO, acupuncturist

T0043040

"*Radical Healership* is the book that astrologers, tarot readers, counselors, and other healing practitioners need. It is a complex and succinct book … [that] gives good advice from an experienced healer about how to start a practice. On a deeper level, it goes over the complexities of being working class and yearning to survive; the ways that healing becomes a profession for those left out of the traditional labor market; and what it means to heal as a job without wanting to make it a job. This is a book that embraces you."

—ALICE SPARKLY KAT, author of *Postcolonial Astrology*

"For those of us trying to survive under capitalism as untraditional therapists and counselors, *Radical Healership* is full of practical advice and hard-earned wisdom. Reading this book feels like being welcomed into a growing web of creative practitioners who are bravely shaping the future of our healing professions in a direction that we desperately need."

—SASCHA ALTMAN DUBRUL, MSW, counselor, cofounder of The Icarus Project, and author of *Maps to the Other Side*

"I am making a container now," Laura Northrup writes, "I invite any unhelpful energies to leave." This simple establishment of ritual space is felt in the whole reading experience—Northrup guides her fellow healers through the steps of developing a healing practice, returning always to the necessity of healing ourselves. Her personal stories serve as examples of the courageous self-understanding that are the essential foundation of our work."

—LAURA LAMB BROWN-LAVOIE, poet, herbalist, and doula

"Written in a style that is simultaneously sophisticated and approachable, this book can help any practitioner—from the newbie to the long-established healer—create vision and coherence in their life's work. No matter what art or discipline of healing you practice, or want to practice, there is something here for you."

—ANNA HOWLAND, psychotherapist

"*Radical Healership* is a gift to healers. If you want to walk the brave path to develop your unique medicine and offer it to those who need it, this book is for you. Laura Northrup shows you how to take care of your financial, spiritual, and emotional needs as you stay true to your radical values. Get ready to feel as if you're in a deep conversation with a wise mentor who always tells you the truth."

—ANNIE SCHUESSLER, host of the podcast *Rebel Therapist*

"*Radical Healership* outlines in straightforward and engaging prose the emotional blocks I spent years stumbling over while building my practice into a viable livelihood. If I'd had this insight available to me when I started, I think I would've made the same progress in five months that wound up taking me five years."

—CHAIKUNI WITAN, Shipibo Medicine Practitioner

"Finally, a deeply thoughtful book that addresses the complex ethical, political, and spiritual dimensions of building a sustainable practice amidst late-stage capitalism and dire environmental reckoning. Laura's words offer nuanced support as we grapple with how to offer our essential services in this critical moment."

—PHILLIPPE CITRINE, MFT, Generative Somatics Coach, founder of the Peacock Course private practice training for trans, queer, and social justice healers

"This highly readable book fits well into a universally accessible, radical anti-capitalist, anti-colonial, modern feminist tradition. Northrup's voice is entirely her own and is unflinchingly REAL—intersectionally attuned, purposefully confessional, often gloriously blunt, and intentional—with clear frameworks for healing. While the focus may technically be aimed toward those who are establishing healing practices, in reality this book is an essential read for anyone who cares for others and wants to do so with greater compassion and understanding. This is a self-help book for the helpers."

—JOHN MINK, social studies teacher and editor of *Teaching Resistance*

"Northrup's personal stories, professional anecdotes, radical know-how, and fiercely compassionate outlook inspired me to see and nurture parts of myself that are critical to my healing practice. This book captures the essence of what it takes to survive and thrive as a healing professional—no matter what point you are at in your journey as a healer."

—LEIA FRIEDWOMAN, MS, Psychedelic Integration Facilitator and host of the podcast *The Psychedologist*

radical
healership

How to Build a Values-Driven Healing Practice in a Profit-Driven World

LAURA MAE NORTHRUP

North Atlantic Books
Huichin, unceded Ohlone land
aka Berkeley, California

Published by
North Atlantic Books
Huichin, unceded Ohlone land
aka Berkeley, California

Cover design by Jess Morphew
Cover art © Rucula/Shutterstock.com
Book design by Happenstance Type-O-Rama

Printed in the United States of America

Radical Healership: How to Build a Values-Driven Healing Practice in a Profit-Driven World is sponsored and published by North Atlantic Books, an educational nonprofit based in the unceded Ohlone land Huichin (aka Berkeley, CA), that collaborates with partners to develop cross-cultural perspectives, nurture holistic views of art, science, the humanities, and healing, and seed personal and global transformation by publishing work on the relationship of body, spirit, and nature.

North Atlantic Books' publications are distributed to the US trade and internationally by Penguin Random House Publishers Services. For further information, visit our website at www.northatlantic books.com.

Library of Congress Cataloging-in-Publication Data

Names: Northrup, Laura, 1981– author.
Title: Radical Healership : how to build a values-driven healing practice in a profit-driven World / Laura Northrup.
Description: Berkeley, California : North Atlantic Books, [2022]
    Includes bibliographical references and index.
Identifiers: LCCN 2021019788 (print) | LCCN 2021019789 (ebook) | ISBN 9781623175993 (trade paperback) | ISBN 9781623176006 (ebook)
Subjects: LCSH: Medicine—Philosophy. | Alternative medicine. | Healing—Practice.
Classification: LCC R723 .N67 2022 (print) | LCC R723 (ebook) | DDC 610.1—dc23
LC record available at https://lccn.loc.gov/2021019788
LC ebook record available at https://lccn.loc.gov/2021019789

1 2 3 4 5 6 7 8 9 KPC 27 26 25 24 23 22

North Atlantic Books is committed to the protection of our environment. We print on recycled paper whenever possible and partner with printers who strive to use environmentally responsible practices.

To life, in all its majestic and unruly forms

*"I have thrown away my lantern,
and I can see the dark."*

—WENDELL BERRY

Contents

Introduction

Humanity needs more healers, because we need more healing. We are living in a global landscape defined by endless war, rampant violence, horrific racism, ongoing genocide, unending sexism, mass incarceration, countless personal traumas, and widespread destruction to the natural world that sustains us. The horrors of our injustices impact the earth, our communities, our families, and our relationships with ourselves.

We live in an era wherein healing practitioners must not only hone their craft to provide a service, but somehow also need to master the art of surviving capitalism. These are two wildly different skill sets and I wrote this book to help you do both.

We cannot live in a loving world without healers. We will not survive our own coping mechanisms without healers. We will never see justice without healers. We are collectively too far past the point of no return. We need help. Healing is as integral to a human life as the simple daily acts of eating food, drinking water, and breathing air. You do it regularly, when needed. We are complex emotional and spiritual beings. Healing is not a singular act, employed after a painful event. It is a way of life and a manner in which we engage in the ongoing upkeep and transformation needed to survive this life and be well. *Suffering is inevitable, and healing is essential.*

As you read this book you will understand how much I believe in the power of intentions. The intention of this book is to inspire you to find the path toward offering healing work in a way that sustains you to do it for a lifetime. My hope is that the things you learn in this book will allow you to be one single part of an enormous collective journey to end injustice and normalize personal and intergenerational healing at every level of our lives.

Whether you have never questioned your commitment to this path or have struggled at each moment to feel confident that you can do it, this book is for you.

So, here's the deal: I am an anti-capitalist healing practitioner and I wrote a self-help book for other healing practitioners about how to run a practice. However, the job and business aspect of being a healing practitioner is inseparable from the spiritual and personal work required to walk this path. For that reason this book explores what it means to do this work and what it means to exist in a capitalist structure as the backdrop to your practice. It's a tricky thing to despise capitalism and want to run a successful practice. Most healing practitioners find this dilemma surfacing at some point in their careers. You may not identify as anti-capitalist but still find yourself averse to "marketing," "branding," and "selling" yourself. You may question what it means to offer healing while operating in an economic system that deeply wounds humanity.

This is a holistic look at what it takes to be a healing practitioner. Practicing healing work is not a job or a career; it is a path. Like an athlete, you will spend your life honing the skills inside of you, to offer up the medicine that is your services. This book is for you if you are answering a calling and you would choose this path regardless of whether you were paid for it or not. This book is not a laundry list of goals to check off that lead you to becoming a financially stable practitioner, because that list doesn't exist. People who are successful in what they do, who love their lives, who do incredible work—they are doing a lot more than a budget and a cookie-cutter marketing plan. They are cultivating an inner world and an outer expression of that world that supports healing and creates an exchange that sustains their own lives. Earning money is not a life goal; it is something you do because you exist within capitalism. You could be very financially successful while being so spiritually and emotionally deprived that you question your desire to live this life.

I am not here to tell you how to exploit anyone. I am not here to tell you how to work four hours a week and be a billionaire. And I am not going to offer you a magical escape route from society or a secret marketing tactic or anything that isn't based in the reality that we live in late-stage capitalism—which is a global culture of violence and exploitation that requires you to work and charge money for your services. The fantasy that one can work only minimally but be financially stable is based in the exploitation of others (who do the work you are not doing, for less money). This book is about finding integrity amid a global culture of greed.

Healers, medicines, and healing—what do these words really mean? Healing is a process of change, wherein something becomes well again or is sustained for a bit longer. The entity receiving healing could be a plant, a human, or the soil under your feet—all of these things can be wounded, can need mending, can receive some healing and thus be sustained and well for longer. Many beings or forces can be healers. Plants can be healers, time can be a healer, and you can be a healer. When you take on that role, you commit yourself to some level of care concerning the wounds of other beings. In this process you become someone who can discern pain. You assess those you work with and see that the alcohol causes a wound, that the childhood abuse causes a wound, and the pesticides cause wounds. When they look hard enough, most healing practitioners awaken to the reality that the very system we live in is causing a wound. You might not think of yourself as "political" or "anti-capitalist," but committing your life to understanding what causes the wound and what heals it opens your eyes to injustice.

You may be an acupuncturist, an intuitive, a tarot reader, a witch, an herbalist, an astrologer, a social worker, a habitat restorer, a sexological bodyworker, a healing voice instructor, a breathworker, a meditation teacher, a sacred medicine guide, a psychotherapist, or any category of healing practitioner. Regardless of what you call your service or how you label your identity, you are someone who is carrying a lineage that has existed and been essential to the survival of our collective humanity since the beginning of time: a healer. You have sacred gifts that you want to offer the world. And this world needs you. You want to be part of the solution to wounding, not the creator of it. To do this, you need to sustain yourself and be well enough to steward others through their pain.

So, what *am* I going to offer you? This book will walk you through the best ways that I know how to support you in being in the highest integrity possible while also existing in the reality of our shared world. I want to help you do the incredible healing work you are here to do. In order to do that you need to love yourself, you need to love the truth more than you love protecting your own ego, you need to love others, and you need to do a shit ton of work—which we will break down step by step in this book. You also need to work with the people you were meant to work with—and that does not mean anyone who happened to look at the contact page on your website and spend thirty seconds writing you an email. You need to work with the people who allow you to do your best work and who help you to remain inspired, dedicated, and offering the services you were meant to offer.

There is a medicine inside of you that is what you bring to this world and to the people you will accompany in their healing. That medicine is most potent when it is in its purest form and not cut by an intermediary along the way. Whatever you have endured in this life, whatever you have had to wade through to get here, it has enriched and informed your medicine, but you will need to work through those hardships to purify and refine your medicine so others can receive it. You have probably already done a lot of work, and this book will invite you to do more. But the other side of that work is running a smooth "business," which nourishes you and the people you serve, while you are fulfilled by a meaningful life and healing practice.

Most businesses fail because of emotional and spiritual blocks. You might call it "bad financial management" or "poor administrative skills," but when we look closer it is so much more. When people are struggling to run a practice, I start to wonder: Did you ask for help when you needed it? Did you admit that you were struggling and humbly learn new skills? Did you charge enough to earn an adequate income and have self-sustaining boundaries? Did you live in scarcity and run yourself into the ground working with people who were not a good fit for you? Did you turn away work because you felt you were "too good" for it and it challenged your self-esteem? Did your unhealed wounds start to run your practice?

This book explores the ways that our egos, personal wounding, and societal wounding inform our abilities to be sustained healing practitioners. The answer to each of the aforementioned questions lies in personal-growth work. Running a practice and being a healing practitioner is vulnerable, hard work. It requires you to grow throughout your life.

Oppression is real. When I talk about working through your material and liberating yourself, I mean in whatever way is possible. You are not responsible to single-handedly transform systems of oppression that target and oppress you. Being the target of white supremacy, patriarchy, religious persecution, transphobia, ableism, classism, and other forms of oppression impacts the ability to build a sustainable practice. While many books on building a practice celebrate the promise of class mobility and imply that working hard or working *smarter* will free you of the financial impacts of any of the above-listed oppressions, the reality is far more complex. If oppression was surmountable simply through labor, we would all be free. However, in any circumstance the question is: What *can* I do? Is there any way to be more in yourself, more loving, more liberated, more alive, more resilient, or more restful than what the first impression seems to offer? This book takes a stern look at personal responsibility while deeply acknowledging that being the target of systemic oppression is not your fault.

In 2012 I spent a weekend learning from Eduardo Duran, author of *Healing the Soul Wound,* that transformed the way I think about being a healing practitioner. Whenever I talk about "finding your song" or "singing your song," I am referencing the learning I received from Eduardo. He was sharing about his process as a psychologist. He shared about being in a Western professional context and learning Jungian theory. Then he shared about how that transformed as he worked with Indigenous community. He explained that in a Western context, we go to school and we learn to regurgitate the songs of the people who came before us. We are assigned papers where we quote the theories of others, where we demonstrate that we know *their song,* that we can go and sing *their songs* and perform *their theories of healing.* But you have a medicine in you: and that is your song. This book is about supporting you to sing your own song. I will share knowledge and offer you guidance, but there is a medicine in you that needs its own tune, its own voice.

Heeding the Call

I have always loved self-help books. In my later teen years I got my hands on a copy of *The Dance of Anger* and studied it with more diligence than the SATs ever got. Don't get me wrong—I was a normal teenager who thought the title of the book was extremely uncool and I hid it from everyone in my life, but nonetheless I was hungry for it. At that time, I was also a burgeoning overfunctioning, codependent workaholic who blackout drank on the weekends. It's hard to think back to my teenage mind and even muster a strongly formed sense of what I must have thought therapy was, but I certainly had some kind of idea and wished I could try it. Self-help books were my affordable and private alternative. I also had this strange feeling that I wanted to *be* a therapist. But when you find yourself waking up in the morning, blankly uncertain of how you got home, putting the pieces of last night's puzzle together with random convenience store receipts from your pockets while bottom-shelf liquor burns a hole in your stomach ... it's hard to feel proud of your hunch that you would make a "great therapist."

We all have gifts, but sometimes those gifts are buried very deep under pain, remnants of unbearable trauma, systemic oppressions, and the daily coping strategies of our lives. It takes bravery and dedication to finally put the hazmat suit on and dive to the bottom. I knew that people often said they felt that they could "tell me anything." I knew that spending hours thinking about the intricacies of interpersonal dynamics and the nature of humanity never bored me. I knew that I was deeply passionate about change and growth. But needless to say: becoming a therapist was a long way out.

In the United States we live in a culture that struggles to process shame, which in turn creates citizens who mirror the cultural difficulties. There aren't many examples of leaders or public figures apologizing, acknowledging mistakes, or even just accepting that something did not go as planned (despite a plethora of situations that warrant such actions). We are focused on success and obsessed with genius, prodigy, and exceptionalism. This makes for a hard time stepping into your self and following your dreams.

Have you ever found yourself not trying something new because you were afraid you would not immediately excel at it? Or have you found yourself following a path because you were decently skilled at it from the start, even if you aren't passionate about it? These are common issues in a world where we aren't taught how to process shame, normalize failure, and normalize learning. Learning implies that you do not yet know or are not yet formed in your skill set. We have become so culturally obsessed with success and productivity that we don't comfortably allow ourselves to be lost, to be in paradoxes that require creativity to resolve; ultimately, being overly focused on success challenges our ability to explore. And exploration is a spiritual necessity in the path toward living a fulfilling life. It takes some practice, but letting yourself be humbled by failure and learn the lessons it has to offer is what often takes you to the next step in life.

There was a time in my life when I was living for praise instead of passion. However, it was doing something I was absolutely terrible at and received no praise for that changed the course of my life. In my mid-twenties I started to train as an aerialist. I spent five days a week training, climbing up ropes, learning tricks on trapeze, rolling around on mats, and accruing injuries that still hurt today. At the risk of being a cliché, I was doing the stuff people do to "find themselves." I trained with several other people who had started around the same time I did. Despite the fact that I trained very hard and said I really wanted to succeed and be a skilled aerialist, I was never as good as anyone else. I never performed, I was always a step behind the people I was surrounded by, and in most cases many steps behind. I felt very badly about this and wanted to quit many times. I could not believe how hard I was training and not getting much in return. I really took that as a sign of something wrong with me and felt ashamed of myself. Then one day I was in a class with a teacher who was trying to figure out why I could not do a particular move. Others were noticing my lack of progress and were equally perplexed by it. I was embarrassed and quickly explained to the teacher that the issue was that I wasn't strong enough yet, while I silently hoped she would wander away. She told me to climb up a rope, curl myself into a ball, and just hold myself there. So I did that. I climbed about five feet into the air, curled my body around a two-inch-thick cotton rope, and just held myself, like a little egg on a string. It burned, because it takes quite a bit of strength to hold yourself on a rope, with no foothold, just pure muscle. After some time she looked at me and said, "It's not a physical issue. You are definitely strong enough; you are just afraid." Wow. She had this way of saying things in the most blunt and unembellished manner. Looking back, I suspect she may have been a Sagittarius. I felt humiliated to have another human see how much my fears held me back, along with the onlooking milieu-style audience of the rest of the class. They could see how my anxiety manifested into the most mundane aspects of my life. I went home from the class just as unskilled as I had been before it.

The experience got me thinking. I realized I didn't trust my body. I didn't trust the strength that I actually had. This could have been an experience where I blamed the teacher—she wasn't teaching me well enough, or she was too blunt—or I could have found some other way to avoid sitting in my own failure (and yes, these thoughts did cross my mind momentarily). However, at that point in my life, I was so sick of being unsatisfied that I just sat in the failure and made a little nest there. Even though I had dedicated endless hours of my time to this craft, I was so afraid of falling, screwing up, getting hurt, looking silly, and being seen as mediocre that I was actually preventing myself from even reaching the goal. If I was going to succeed, I needed to be willing to not know and still try, to be in the mediocrity of being a clumsy and hopeful beginner. I know how you probably think this story is going to end: that I marched back into that studio, surrendered to the process, failed countless more times, and trained even harder until I nailed that move ... but that is actually very far from what happened.

I started to think more deeply about what I was spending five days a week doing and I wondered: Why am I doing this? Is this THE THING I want to train for? I did not trust the strength that I actually had, but was *this* the profound life path that I was going to face my fears to excel in? I looked around at my peers and realized the reason other people were far more successful than I was: they actually wanted this, they wanted to be professional aerialists, they wanted to do this way more than I did, and they were willing to risk failure in order to get there. If I was truly being honest with myself, I wanted to be a psychotherapist. The gifts that I was given in this lifetime were not intended to entertain people; they were intended to transform people. And the longer that I did not listen to that gift, the longer I would be perplexed by my dissatisfaction with the life I was creating. Becoming a therapist was the thing I was truly afraid to do and holding myself back from, not a dance trick. So, I quit training and went to grad school.

It was a valuable experience to be terrible at something. Before that time in my life, I couldn't be in contact with what I desired out of life because I felt imprisoned by what I was good at. Praise had to be protected at all costs. Suffering a reality of zero praise allowed me to break free from praise-seeking.

* * *

Somewhere inside of you is a flame that lights your path. It may be quite dim at the moment, barely the flicker of a match. Or it could be strong and radiantly filling the room. It could be a crackling whisper of a spark that you can barely hear in your quietest moments, or it could be the steady whirring of fire so hot that anything in its path will burn. Your task is to *look* and *listen* and *believe* it. When we push away our gifts, our passions, our desires ... we live a half life at best. Asking yourself what your path is takes courage. It demonstrates an interest in truth over comfort. You have to be willing to fail to succeed. So, what I want to ask you is: what is this path that brews inside of you? I am not asking you what your parents think your path is, not what your friends would approve of, not what society has instructed you to be, and not what you think you are capable of. I am not asking what you went to college for, or what you have spent the last twenty years dedicated to. I am not asking what you think you deserve. I am not even asking you what you think you can do right now with where you are in your life at this very moment. I am asking: if you can manage to work through whatever it takes to get there, what are you meant to do in this lifetime? When you imagine being an elder, looking back at your life, what will you have done that lets you know that you lived this life and your gifts to your fullest potential?

To desire something is to be hungry, to want, to need. It is tied up in the vulnerable pursuit of pleasure. Desire implies a certain sense of self-esteem. It is the audacity to believe that you are worthy of the time, the attention, the commitment, that your dreams are meaningful. It is not a standing ovation; it is showing up to train when you barely have skills. It is not an experience of being satiated, met, contained, or accomplished. It's the rawness of not having, yet wanting. It's a risky thing to admit what you really want and to be in contact with desire.

Desire is also a powerful tool. Hungering for something produces the motivation to reach for it. However, when a strong feeling goes unnamed or unexpressed, it typically finds an indirect, sideways route toward expression or resolve. It is a dangerous thing to deny desire, because it can produce unconscious manipulative behaviors (as a means to get the desire met without asking directly) and it can produce self-destructive behaviors (as a means to numb the desire and disconnect from it). In worst-case scenarios, this can result in hurting yourself or others. In the realm of your life path and healing practice, it can result in profound disappointments. How would you feel to look back in thirty years and know that you did not live from your passions, that you let the flame go out?

In the United States, we live in a cultural landscape of shame. Desire is attacked at one of its most sacred locations, your sexuality. The policing of sexual desire is vast and pervasive, but can be seen in the simple, yet prevalent views that queerness is sinful and that sex is only for procreation and not pleasure. To be shamed at the level of our sexuality is to be systematically disempowered. In Audre Lorde's essay "The Uses of the Erotic: The

Erotic as Power," she makes the point that in a patriarchal society, erotic energy is viewed as simply just sex,[1] whereas she asserts that erotic energy is a place of personal and political power. Wilhelm Reich, who was a Freudian analyst and somatic psychology theorist, wrote a book called *The Mass Psychology of Fascism*, in which he explores the human body as an essential location of social control for fascism. He says, "the goal of sexual suppression is that of producing an individual who is adjusted to the authoritarian order and will submit to it in spite of all misery and degradation."[2] Desire is power, and the suppression of it creates a state of disempowerment.

Wanting and needing are also attacked on the primal level of survival. This can be seen in the oppressive structures of classism and white supremacy. Dominant US cultural narratives hold poverty as a personal failure, rather than a result of the exploitation inherent in capitalism, systemic oppression, and lack of social services. To be financially struggling is so shameful that many US citizens live in constant debt in order to look the part and to pretend that they can afford a more expensive lifestyle. We let people live and die on the street, sleeping on sidewalks, unshielded from the elements. Financially impoverished refugees seeking political asylum to save their lives are called "illegal" and put into detention-center prisons. White supremacy weaponizes need and desire against people of color. There is little dignity afforded to those who are in the greatest of need, as dominant society shuns, shames, and criminalizes that level of vulnerability and dependency while simultaneously being the creators of it. Even if you have been spared living in a high state of need, it is the messaging adrift in the air you breathe. Much of white culture and wealth culture is about not knowing one's self, but rather focusing on power, money, and entertainment as the substance of self; white supremacy is against intimacy, which includes the self-intimacy required to discern one's true needs. Starting a business, taking risks in your life path, going into student-loan debt—the anxiety of failure, need, and dependency underlies it all.

If you have suffered or currently suffer through poverty, listening to the gifts in yourself or following your passion and desire might feel dangerous and grief-filled. Drumming up the shame of needing and not having, it can feel painful to want. But stopping yourself before you start will only result in merging with the neglect that society forces onto you. With the risk of trying comes the potential for having your needs met. If you are someone who has lived with wealth privilege, part of that privilege may include numbing out to the intolerable dissonance of you having more than enough while someone else is struggling to survive. But numbness is a disconnection from your humanity that perpetuates oppression and encourages apolitical approaches to healing. It may feel shameful to want, it may feel wrong for you to have a path all to your own, while so many still suffer. But you are not contributing to the end of anyone's suffering by remaining impotent and guilty.

When you explore your path, especially in a realm that relates to your financial livelihood and the passion that drives you, it is a reasonable response for fear of failure, rejection, disappointment, and shame to start creeping in. It is reasonable, as Lorde and Reich have pointed out, to feel disempowered and controlled by social norms, or so repressed and ashamed about your desires that they are hard to admit. For that reason, I want to offer you some protection: you don't have to tell anyone your thoughts on this today or even next year. For ten years I kept it a secret inside myself that I wanted to be a therapist. Here is who I don't want you to keep it a secret from: yourself.

* * *

When you ask yourself about your path, you can go from the vast and profound to the minute and ordinary. You could be exploring if you want to be a healing practitioner at all or if your schedule will include working nights; if you want to go into solo private practice or work on a team. The point of this moment in your process is to be clear and honest with yourself about your wants, needs, and gifts. Making decisions about your path or your business based on what others have done, based on what is "normal," or based on what you think you should do leaves an opening for substantial burnout. You are the one who will be living your life every day, so make your best attempt to live in a way that suits you.

When I first started my therapy practice I thought running a successful business meant that I couldn't be myself. I tried to dress in ways that I thought therapists "should" dress. I tried to tone down my personality and be softer and more graceful. I also thought that very good therapists don't have too many boundaries, because they are so loving, accepting, and self-less. *What the hell was I thinking?* That is an exhausting way to live. It takes a lot of energy to stop being yourself and try to be someone else. And you definitely cannot do your best work under those circumstances. There was even a point when I considered changing careers because I just hated the stress of becoming someone else every day. The medicine that you create in yourself, as a healer, is from your lived experiences and *that* is what you use to support people. *That* is your song. *That* is why people come to see you. Not because you look like someone else, or you trained with a particular person, or your website has a great design. You can sing someone else's song for only so long until you have to embrace your own. Being a healing prac-titioner is hard work and you have to create a practice that you can thrive in or you risk burnout. Before I could build a sustainable practice, I had to truly confront the ways I didn't love who I was, and how that informed this constant pressure to be someone else. The truth is: despite my best efforts to be a quiet, graceful therapist who eloquently offers finely worded insights in soft, flowing sweaters—I am loud, silly, I get to the point, and I do most of that in leopard-print pumps and neon hair. No one has ever described me as graceful, and I have the same number of needs as any other human; now I can honestly say: I love that about myself.

For some time before I became a therapist, I was an experimental film-maker. I spent long hours animating and drawing, and even longer hours editing on a computer. Experimental filmmakers aren't known for raking in the big ones, and so toward the end of my filmmaking career, I worked at a small Christian café making stale-bread sandwiches, terrible coffee, and minimum wage. Times were tough for the café, since it was mainly frequented only by people from a single church in a small town. Why they hired me remains a mystery. I was the only employee not associated with the church (or any organized religion) and I think my employment might have been part of a larger attempt to rebrand and to inspire a cus-tomer base outside of the church. My paychecks would bounce often, and most of the slow hours behind the counter were spent giving the owner emotional support about her post-divorce dating life and dodging near-constant sexual harassment and degradation from my "boss" (the owner's eighteen-year-old son).

Because of my work editing my own films, I started to pick up video-editing jobs on the side at the local college, which afforded me the part-time work to cope with my bouncing checks from the Christian café. Quite the opposite of being a captive audience to the café owners: editing was solitary. My coworker was a computer and our conversations never got personal, sticking mainly to swearing at software for crashing and long wait times for a render. If I was working on an interesting project, I would watch fascinating authors lecture about things I wished I was studying. And if I was working on a boring project, I was naturally quite bored.

When I finally came to terms with the need to take more personal responsibility for my destiny, I did an exercise. It's an exercise in dreaming and desire:

I made a list of things that I loved about former jobs and a list of things that I hated.

The list was exhaustive. It included things as small as what time I had to wake up in the morning and as complex as how the work translated into a sense of meaning. I wrote that as much as I loved film, I hated sitting in front of a computer. And even though I had absolutely no confidence in my ability to run my own business, I hated being an employee, subjected to whatever my "boss" wanted to discuss that day. I despised being in a role where someone could sexually harass me every day and the only option for stopping it was to quit. It felt terrible to admit, but it was true: I wanted tons of control. At that time in my life I was still trying to pretend that I was "laid-back" and could get along with anyone. I would watch my boss make imprudent business decisions and silently feel ashamed of myself that I thought I had a more organized and sensible approach. *Who was I to think things like that? I made minimum wage, for Christ's sake.* Saturated with internalized sexism and classism, I was socialized to doubt myself, to pretend I wasn't as good at things, and above all I was never to challenge an authority figure's methods.

I made a second set of lists that consisted of three categories:

Category 1: everything you absolutely CANNOT have in your life path

Category 2: everything you absolutely MUST have in your life path

Category 3: things you want or don't want, but could be flexible about

We exist in capitalism, which relies on the exploitation of labor to amass wealth. What that looked like in my life was: I worked just as hard as or harder than my boss, but my boss made more money. I was done with this. And I didn't want to be the boss either. I never want to be in a power dynamic where anyone feels uncomfortable being themselves in my presence or saying "no" to me because they fear for their job and their survival. More power to you if you want to be a radical boss; it just wasn't for me.

The category-based lists were a way of organizing and refining everything I had written down regarding what I loved and hated about former jobs. So, instead of recording a specific memory about what I cherished in a former position, I would put a line in such as: *I must work in an environment free of sexual harassment.* I will add that just because you make a list of things you want and don't want doesn't mean that is what life will offer you. Intentions are different from outcomes, yet they still matter. Sexual harassment and gender-based harm have not ended in my life because I recognized a need for them to end. Most forms of oppression are experiences that we navigate throughout our lives, and it can be hard to take a strong stance against experiencing them when we know that they will continue to occur. Still, I want to encourage you to be clear on what you truly want, because staying connected to truth is healing in itself. And if it is not possible to create a work environment with minimal oppression, then be sure to minimize it in the places where you have more choice: friendships and community.

Making lists like this isn't about coming to a final answer immediately. This is a step on your path. These lists are a structured exercise in knowing yourself more completely. When you make your lists, you may find that they produce more questions, which result in a need to explore and do further research. I had a lot of life experience (i.e., terrible employment situations) to draw from in making these lists. If you don't have as much, it is also possible that you are in a place in life where you need to play and explore before you can answer these kinds of questions. If this is the case, you may find some ease in accepting that and moving forward with it, rather than trying to force yourself to be ready to make a huge life commitment. Going to graduate school, attending trainings, apprenticing under a mentor, doing the work to build a business—these things take immense effort and when the going gets tough, it is made easier if it is what you really want to be doing (remember my sad aerialist days).

In addition to making these lists is the simple task of being with your own truth. For many, clarity comes through conversation with others: close people, inspiring people, ancestors, plants, or spirit. For others clarity comes by going inward through meditation, journaling, and deep thinking. I find that my best thoughts don't happen while I am staring at my phone or tired. Many theorists and creators throughout time have attested to this, reporting that their best work comes in dreams, on walks, or while taking the time to let the mind wander. I am guessing that goes the same for you. So, put away the screens, stop searching the internet for ten-point lists on successful businesses, and call a friend or go for a walk. Give yourself time. This is a process that will result in choices that guide the rest of your life. Can there be joy in this exploration? Can you be curious about who you are now and who you will become?

If you find yourself wildly uncomfortable with exploring your potential life path, explore your discomfort first. Self-exploration starts with what is *now* and where *we are at,* not with where we *wish* we were at. Exploration is a state of not yet knowing and it's a state of dreaming. If you hate this exercise, if you feel afraid to be in a state of not knowing: explore that. There is wisdom in resistance. Perhaps your resistance to this exploration has some knowledge in it that needs your attention.

Failure is a generous teacher when you surrender to being a student. While you are exploring the depths of what successfully being on your path could look like, let yourself explore the depths of what failure could look like. And really ask yourself: What is actual failure? Is it trying something and having to make adjustments along the way? Is it admitting that you cannot do this alone and need help? Is it the hard work of having to go back and correct mistakes? Is it the emotions you will experience when things go wrong? Is it deciding in ten years that you have a different end goal and that your life path is changing? We are a culture that emphasizes shame in relationship to "failure." However, even the smallest act of failure teaches us things: what we want to be different, what needs to change, what limits need to be accepted, what needs attention, how to say "I am sorry," how to do better next time. So, do you fear failure? Or do you fear what you will feel about yourself when failure happens? Part of getting what you want out of life is learning to be humbled and motivated by things that go wrong.

EXERCISES AND EXPERIENTIALS

CHAPTER 1

At the end of each chapter in this book you will find exercises and experientials for further exploration. There are many ways to build a deeper relationship with yourself and these are just suggestions. If the provided format doesn't feel accessible to you, find a way to connect to these inquiries in whatever way makes sense for your process. A writing prompt could become a conversational prompt. A body scan could become an expressive arts process. A conversational exercise could become a tarot spread. Follow what you know about how you learn and grow best.

1.1 *Writing*

1. Make a list of things you have loved about former jobs, volunteer positions, and educational settings.

2. Make a list of things you have strongly disliked or hated about former jobs, volunteer positions, and educational settings.

3. If you have less than twenty entries on each list, keep working on it and find at least twenty things you can point to on each list. These don't have to be profound; the idea is to really let yourself be rigorous and thorough with the exercise.

4. After you have finished these lists, take a moment to look them over with curiosity. What stands out to you? Did anything surprise you? How was it for you to write these things down?

1.2 *Writing*

Make a list with three columns or categories. This is a process of dreaming. Your feelings about these things may change or you may end up needing to compromise on them, but the first step is just being honest with yourself about what you hope for.

Category 1: write down everything you feel you absolutely CANNOT have in your life path.

Category 2: write down everything you feel you absolutely MUST have in your life path.

Category 3: write down things you want or don't want, but could be flexible about.

1.3 *Writing*

1. What does failure look like to you? How do you feel about yourself when you "fail" at something? What has failure taught you?

2. What does success look like to you? How do you feel when you "succeed" at something? What has success taught you?

3. What is it like for you to desire or need something?

4. How have privilege and oppression impacted your relationship to knowing and accepting yourself or your path?

1.4 *Body Scan*

1. Look over your lists of things you have loved and hated about previous work, and choose one item that has a memory attached to it.

2. Find a quiet place to do a body scan. You can be sitting, standing, lying down, or walking (though most people find it is easier to do a body scan in stillness). Choose somewhere contained, where you can close the door or won't be interrupted by other people or electronics.

3. Once you are settled, bring to mind your memory and the thing you do or don't like. Take as long as you need to really get into the feeling of the memory.

4. Now let your focus be on your body. Start with your breath and take note of how deep or wide it is. This practice is not about changing your breathing; it is about noticing what is.

5. When you are ready, start at the top of your head and work your way down your body, *feeling the inside of your self.* Notice the sensations, be they discomfort, tension, lightness, excitement. Work your way through your head, your torso, your pelvis, your arms, your legs, and all the way to your feet. There are parts of our bodies we often avoid—parts that feel sexual, parts that have been shamed. But those are your body too, so see if there is room to notice your chest, your belly, your guts, your genitals, and your thighs. Whenever you are done, bring your sense back to the external world.

6. Be curious: What are these sensations? Can you discern the difference between anxiety and excitement? They can feel quite similar. Can you feel the difference between numbness and contentedness? They can feel quite similar.

7. A body scan in itself is a great way to sit deeper with how you feel at any given moment or about a particular thing. However, it is also a way to familiarize yourself with what the cues are that indicate something works and truly resonates with you versus when something external needs to be different or there is a need for healing. After your body scan make a mental note, write down what you learned, or share it with someone. You are building a reservoir of knowledge about yourself; find a way to keep track of and engage with this information over time.

8. If you need a voice walking you through this exercise, many prerecorded body scan instructions exist online and are accessible through a simple search or you can make a recording of your own voice giving instructions and listen to that.

Why?

In 2007, I started seeing a therapist named Elizabeth Bolles. She was studying Somatic Experiencing at the time and was enrolled in a somatic psychology doctorate program. She offered classes on somatic theory and embodiment that were open to her clients. My interest in the field of somatic study ignited through my relationship with her. This was my first meaningful relationship with a therapist.

In April of 2008, while enrolled in one of her classes, my father passed away from lung cancer. I had a tormented relationship with him, and his death was simultaneously devastating and liberating. Two days later, Elizabeth called to inform me that she would no longer be able to see me for individual sessions, as she was diagnosed with pancreatic cancer. It had already metastasized, spreading to many of her internal organs.

There was no funeral for my father, as he did not want one. My younger brother flew in from his station in Iraq and we went to Onalaska, Texas, to say our goodbyes. He wanted us to see our father, so the funeral home director wheeled out his frozen, naked body, covered by a bedsheet. I stood staring at the harmless, ice-cold shell of a man whom I feared, hated, and longed for connection with. I did not grieve his death; I grieved the death of my dream that someday he would be a loving parent who gave me all of the affection and attention I needed. He died the way he lived: dishonest and evasive; he hid his diagnosis from me, telling me only after the doctors were clear that he would not survive. The resulting family dynamics were chaotic and scarring for many.

Elizabeth lived only two more months. We never saw each other again for an individual session. However, during that time she taught her class when she felt well enough. After Elizabeth's diagnosis, class was mostly about being fully present for our last few encounters with an incredible human being. She would talk about what it was like to be dying, to become wholly dependent on others. She described her inability to regulate her own affect. She said it was like becoming a child. We watched as she quickly deteriorated, lost all of her hair, and offered us the powerful gift of witnessing her death and holding her spirit. We would cry and openly express our fears of losing her. She told us that we could use the experience to heal. She encouraged us to stay embodied, feel the depth of the grief, and move through it.

Like my father, she died at home, as commercial developers clear-cut the forest that was her backyard. Her sister, mother, and friends adorned her body with flowers from her garden and held a twenty-four-hour vigil immediately following her death. People were there all night, playing with her cats, eating baked goods, laughing, and crying. The power of attending her vigil was indescribable when I compare it to that of my farewell to my father. It was a gift that few have the power, inner strength, and generosity to give. I was deeply moved, and as instructed by her, I used the experience to foster healing related to the death of my father.

Even in the most painful and tragic moments of her life—watching herself die—she was able to be rooted in the values that guided her life. She watched each of her dreams fade away. She was writing her dissertation. She was an incredible theorist. She would have contributed to the field of ecopsychology and somatic psychology in profound ways. And yet she died young, with two months' notice. There is no rhyme or reason to this. Elizabeth was a person who was so committed to being a healing practitioner that she even offered her death in the service of others. She was not ignoring other aspects of her life, she was not selfless, yet she gave what she felt called to until the very end.

I never asked Elizabeth why she chose this path. Some time after she passed, at her memorial, I listened to her peers, her family, and her other clients talk about her life. And I know what it was like to know her, to be in her presence. She cared more about the truth than anything else. She cared more about depth than about staying palatable. When she told me she could no longer see me for therapy, she didn't mince words or beat around the bush—she just let it be the realest thing that it was: completely devastating and absolutely necessary.

Behind every practitioner is a reason "why" they do this work. Your "why" can be felt in all the things that you do. It is what you orbit around, it informs how you move through the world, and it lays the foundation for what you can offer to others. I am telling you this story about Elizabeth because it exemplifies how healers live (and die) their values, how those can be felt by others, and how their values play a part in facilitating healing. In a sense, this story is also about how all of us, regardless of being in the role of a healer, live and die our values. My father illustrates the ways that one's values can be the opposite of healing: wounding. He wounded the people around him until the bitter end.

Who we end up working with can at times come about in a sacred and mysterious way. I cannot put words to how tragic it was to have my therapist die along with my father, but it was also an incredible gift. It is clear that as humans, we are drawn to others with shared values. I believe that as healers, that is who we do our best work with. That does not mean that you are the same, practice the same religion, or have the same lifestyle. It means that something about the deep spiritual truths you hold is meaningful to the people you work with. Elizabeth and I were very different people. At times I didn't agree with things she said, at times she offended me, and I have had quite a different path than her. Yet, one very clear tenet of how I live my life is that I value speaking what I know to be the truth and embracing the depth and complexity of the human experience—we shared that.

Understanding why you do this work and grounding yourself in that is the spiritual foundation of what will become your concrete and material reality. It is the internal structure that allows you to create a space for others. Being able to communicate the underlying values that inform and guide you is essential in giving the people you work with the information needed to choose you. And it will guide you in choosing them.

Death is a powerful teacher and one of its greatest lessons is about how to live. Our lives feel so permanent until they aren't. We typically imagine that every goodbye will eventually be followed by another hello. When I was fourteen, a guidance counselor at my middle school sat me down to share that a friend of mine had killed himself the night before. She said, "You don't know who will be here tomorrow, so you need to tell them you love them today." She shared a piece of her medicine with me that day, the simple value of expressing love. It is something that I have been able to carry with me all these years since. However, I want to add something from my medicine and values to that: you don't know if *you* will be here tomorrow, so you also need to love yourself today. Letting yourself take the risk to live with integrity and honesty toward yourself and others, to follow the gifts inside of you: do it today. To offer your medicine to the world is a gift. Regardless of that sense that there is always more time, there isn't. My intention isn't to rush you, but to inspire you to use your time wisely. Every great feat is a series of small tasks. Of course, you will not be at the end of your path today just by deciding that you want to live more fully in alignment with your values. However, even in the smallest moments, you can ask yourself: is there any room here to be more myself, to live out these values that I hold so dearly?

It is incredibly vulnerable to choose a healing practitioner to work with. People often come to us in their most painful moments. Trust is an important part of this process, and people will have more ease in discerning whether to trust you if they can feel your underlying beliefs. If you have truly amazing underlying beliefs, but you aren't connected to them, and you don't communicate them in, say, your website or the other ways that you connect to the people you want to work with, people will not be able to *feel you* and will be less likely to work with you. Many healers shy away from letting their personality or uniqueness come through, feeling that they must be like everyone else. However, your personality is a facet of your medicine, and you need people to feel who you are in order for them to comfortably enter a healing relationship with you. Letting your underlying beliefs and personality come through also supports you to work with people who are a good fit for you. No healer is meant to work with every person who happens by. As Simon Sinek points out in his TED Talk "How Great Leaders Inspire Action," if people made choices based on what was offered or how it was offered, they would choose a healing practitioner by typing "life coach" or "astrologer near me" into a search engine and take the first person who comes up. People don't do that, because regardless of whether they articulate it as I am doing, they are interested in the deeper beliefs that you hold.[3]

Your task is to identify why you do this work. This is a deep spiritual question, and the answer may come to you with ease or take some time to emerge. When I went on this journey myself, I first thought of many moments that seemed like they should be my "why." Moments such as when I helped someone else and perhaps even emotionally moved or inspired them, or when a teacher gave me some praise and I felt truly good at something. Although these things were quite meaningful, none of them brought me to a deep, visceral sense of my "why" until I went way back and remembered myself as a kid. The suffering we have endured and subsequently healed is often a road to understanding why one does healing work. Suffering spiritualizes and radicalizes us in ways that wellness cannot. I do not state this to glamorize suffering, but rather so that we understand how it impacts us and shapes who we become. I had a very difficult childhood and in searching for my "why" I remembered what it felt like to be in so much pain, to feel that I was alone and the suffering might never end. When one has no embodied perception of the potential of increased peace that comes with healing, it can feel as though the present lived experience will be eternal. Yet, somehow my kid self kept persisting. I kept getting up every day, going to school, trying to play, reading books, and imagining a different life. At times, I considered suicide, but still, I never gave up hope. The spark inside of me stayed alive, even if it was dim for long periods of time. Why is that? Because some very wise and integral part of me believed and still does believe that liberation is possible. And that is why I do this work. Protest signs and political campaigns and positive memes and other healers can say it to me loud and clear and I agree with them, but the place where I know it is in my heart: that people can survive hardship, that change is possible, that liberation is achievable.

Liberation may not look exactly like what we hope for, but aspects of it are possible. Liberation is not a personal struggle; some of the people who came to my aid in the hardest moments of my life have been people who have struggled and turned back to offer help, refusing to leave others behind. The path toward liberation is a collective struggle that we engage in for the freedom of all, for the freedom of generations to come, freedoms that we may not experience in our own lifetimes.

I don't normally tell people how to feel, but I do want to give you the guidance that when you come into a deeper sense of knowing why you do this work, it should feel emotional or moving. If you find yourself feeling flat about it, feeling like you can't answer this question, or looking to what others think about why healing matters—take the time to keep exploring your personal relationship to this question of "why?" Most healers come to the work through their own wounds. Exploring the most hurt parts of you may help to illuminate this question of why.

You might also ask yourself: What is it that makes you stay on this path? In the most challenging of moments, why did you keep choosing this, rather than throw in the towel? Knowing why you do this work will also buoy you through the hardest parts—and let me tell you: there will be hard moments. Being a healer is anything but easy. It is committing your life to your own healing and being with the raw fucking pain of this world. Each time you come upon another wound in yourself, you will need to address it so that you can continue to serve. We cannot ask the people we work with to engage in healing behaviors or processes that we wouldn't engage in ourselves. The more distant we become from what we offer or what it is like to be the client, the less effective we are. Being a healer is listening to and supporting people through things they can change and things they just have to accept. It is staying present to profoundly disturbing and violent things that humans are capable of. Being a healer requires engaging with the deep spiritual questions of what it means to be a human: to live a life, to suffer, to love, to hate, to desire, to fall ill, to die. Staying grounded in why you do this work is an essential resource to guide you through the most heart-wrenching moments.

I invite you to start writing, praying, meditating, dreaming, and asking yourself: Why am I doing this work? What am I truly here for on this earth?

EXERCISES AND EXPERIENTIALS
CHAPTER 2

2.1 *Reflection*

1. What did you feel while you read this chapter?

2. What memories, if any, emerged?

3. What sensations did you feel in your body? If you are not sure, you can do the body scan exercise from chapter 1.

2.2 *Writing*

1. Which of your life experiences inspired you to be a healer?

2. What gifts do you have that others experience as healing?

3. When you think about the larger impact you are leaving on this planet, what do you want that to be?

4. What do you want your life to say or stand for?

5. Take your answers to these questions and distill them into a sentence or two. Try to capture the essence of why you do this work, without needing to overly explain it.

2.3 *Poem*

1. Creative expression can help the unconscious become more conscious. What follows is a poem to help you get connected with your "why." Fill in the blanks keeping in mind that you can change this or do it differently in the future; for now just write down the first thing that comes to mind. It is a game and there is no need to do it perfectly.

   In my lifetime,

   My imagination has conjured _____.

My body has traveled through _____.

My heart has felt _____.

My gut has told me that _____.

My spirit has guided me to _____.

My compass points toward _____.

My being has held _____.

My story has been about _____.

My fire has been _____.

My song sounds like _____.

My inspirations have been _____.

My breath has felt _____.

My love encompasses _____.

_____ nurtures me.

The Shadow-Why

As I have said, I believe in truth over comfort, so let's talk about what I call your "shadow-why." The shadow-why encompasses all the less-altruistic, unconscious reasons for why you do this work. This is important to understand about yourself, because whatever unconsciously motivates you to do this work will influence how you do it. Additionally, if you do not engage with the more unconscious and wounded parts of yourself, they can hurt the people you work with. You will need to explore and make these parts of yourself as conscious as you can. Healers frequently come into this work from our own wounding and that wounding often comes with very primal responses that can look like entitlement, rage, sorrow, denial, desperation, shame, terror, and self-loathing. As the saying goes: hurt people hurt people. While many of us become more compassionate because of our wounding, we also have the capacity to be harmful or even abusive to others. Most of the time when someone acts in an abusive manner, their internal experience is that they are appropriately protecting themselves from a perceived harm or acting in a just way. When you are in the thick of it, it can be confusing to sort out hurtful, wounded parts from more-grounded behaviors. For this reason, part of understanding the unconscious or less-conscious parts of ourselves often includes taking in feedback from others. Sometimes people give us feedback in very negative ways, especially when it is in response to less-savory parts of ourselves. Taking in feedback doesn't mean uncritically accepting whatever someone else says about you. However, it does mean really considering what someone has offered through their feedback—even if it is given in a harsh way.

It is easy to get wrapped up in one-sided or flat examples of healers or spiritual leaders. Someone like Mother Teresa or the Dalai Lama come to mind (not that they *are* flat, but that they are often *flattened* in how people perceive them). It is important to remember that even if you are a very powerful healer, with striking skill and gifts, you are still always human. That means you are not a saint or a god. The beauty of being human is the ability to be in the full range of human emotions and actions, and that includes the capacity to harm others. However, it is a tricky thing to live in the complexity of being a person who offers healing and also has problems and maybe even acts poorly sometimes. This is not something we talk about very often in our respective healing fields. It will make you a stronger and more effective healer to be honest with yourself about your shortcomings and potential to cause harm. The compassion you give to your own flaws will support you to meet others from a compassionate place.

When it comes to running a practice, our shadow-whys can also create havoc when unchecked. A classic example of this among healing practitioners is overidentification with being a generous caregiver and feeling ashamed to need care (or being highly dissociated from one's own needs). I have listened to countless healers speak poorly of other practitioners for charging a reasonable rate, calling them "greedy" or "uncaring"; meanwhile, the person ascribing these negative ideas to others is barely making their rent, asking their parents for money to cover basic expenses, and refusing to raise their rates or have a sliding scale that is sustainable.

I myself am guilty of a version of this. When I first started as a therapist, I thought it was unfair to deny anyone therapy based on ability to pay. It got to the point that I had a full practice that was all quite low fee. I have reasonable financial management skills, so I wasn't calling in favors to pay my basic expenses, but I was not paying my student loans and the interest grew and grew. When I heard of others who did not even have a sliding scale to speak of—I was appalled! These were clearly people who did not care about injustice; they did not care about the healing that everyone deserves. However, let's take that mindset and pretend for a moment that I held it for the duration of my career. Among a myriad of other financial issues, I would never pay off my student loans and I would probably also never save for retirement. Additionally, if I suffered any type of serious illness or injury, I would not be able to support myself or reasonably take a needed leave of absence from work, and I would probably accrue more medical debt. So, I would be in debt *for the rest of my life* and unable to retire. Justice is not trading suffering for suffering. That is masochism. Yes, everyone deserves access to healing—I truly believe this. However, it is arrogant, falsely omnipotent, and unrealistic to imagine that I, a single human, am going to create such a profound stand for justice that will heal so many people by driving myself into massive, lifelong debt. In this story, I was completely disconnected from my own sense of need and was projecting that need onto my low-income clients. My time would have been better spent creating a reasonable sliding scale and capping it, while helping other therapists and healers to do the same, so that more of us are collectively offering affordable services while still sustaining ourselves.

In the role of healer, we exist in a power position to others who come to us in vulnerable states. This dynamic creates an easy opportunity to project parts of ourselves that we do not love or are not aware of onto the people we work with. Yes, I worked with many low-income individuals, but I myself was low income. I was not in a place to offer the level of generosity that was asked of me. However, I didn't want to know that about myself. I didn't want to be the needy one; I didn't want to be the therapist my colleagues secretly called "greedy" and "uncaring." Part of my shadow-why was wanting to be seen as a generous, principled person who always put the needs of others before my own. However, I have to ask myself: is it healing to project all this need onto the people I work with? The answer is "no." The people I work with are not there to make me feel a certain way; they are not working with me to be used as protection against parts of myself that I do not like.

Am I proud of this story? No. Do I cringe a little telling it to you? Yes. As with uncovering your more altruistic and lovely reasons for doing this work, there is a feeling that comes along with uncovering the layers of your shadow-why. You will know it when you come to it. It feels embarrassing, somewhat shameful, and like something you don't want to put in a book for others to read.

While I was living out my savior fantasy, I did get gentle, supportive feedback from a few peers that I was allowed to charge more and make a sustainable living. However, in more direct and harsh moments, it was clear that some peers thought I was being foolish. As described above, this was not congruent with the wounded narrative I was attached to. Feedback from others gives us so much insight into our unconscious behaviors and beliefs. It was hard to hear, but slowly I started listening to these peers and setting aside my self-righteous ideology. Looking back, it sounds almost absurd that I would be so negligent about my own finances while supporting people to be more thoughtful about theirs, but that is how wounded parts operate. As you are exploring your shadow-why, consider feedback you have received from others and possibly turned away from. It is likely you have had several opportunities to explore these parts of yourself, albeit as veiled, easily ignored, and small reflections from others.

In addition to the one I described above, there are four very common shadow-why scenarios that healers find themselves in. I will give a brief outline of each, including why healers are specifically prone to them, and how they can impact running a sustainable practice. However, you are a unique individual, so remember that these examples are just guides, and your own story is likely far more nuanced and complex.

Wanting to Be Revered and Achieve Success with Ease

A common fantasy is to be a well-known, revered healer, with a thriving practice that requires no work to build, where every person you work with is a good fit. I know this sounds extreme when I lay it out like that; people don't typically articulate this fantasy in such a straightforward way. As with most unconscious or semi-conscious things, it tends to be more visible in the derivative of one's actions and words. Public images of social media healers make this fantasy even more alluring: we see healers and spiritual guides with hundreds of thousands of "followers" on their social media platforms, posting photos that show a happy, luxurious life, and we never see photos of them making a spreadsheet or worrying about their website search engine optimization and conversion rates. The massive amount of work that went into creating this online image and their offerings is invisible. Furthermore, they are revered. We see that people "like" them and their offerings, people "share" their offerings, and we can even see the number of people who do all this "liking." Living in a culture that fetishizes happiness and glorifies fame, wealth, and the perception of endless leisure time—it is not a surprise that any of us fantasize about this kind of life as a solution to our problems, and it is not specific to our respective healing fields.

However, what do you hear underneath this fantasy? Two strong themes emerge: (1) shame is relieved by being revered, and (2) things come easy to one in this fantasy; it is a fantasy where one finally gets a break from hardship. Many healers are people who have suffered from not having enough and having to work hard to survive. This could mean not enough love, not enough attention, or not enough materially, in terms of finances and material well-being. A common fantasy in reaction to intense suffering and not-enoughness is to imagine that there is a life that is possible where there is no suffering, and that you are entitled to that life. Many people strive to get there, as if there is a *there* to get to.

If you are a person who fantasizes that your peers are doing so much better than you, and they are being handed everything and it isn't fair—you might fall into this category. Perhaps you imagine that people should be flocking to you without you doing the work to inspire flocking. Every healer with a successful practice has worked hard to create it. In the years I have spent teaching healers how to build a practice, I have never met anyone who did not suffer in the creation of it. Despite that being the case, I have listened to many a person fret that others are being handed a career and are adored by colleagues while they are being deprived. I can assure you, successful healers work very hard behind the scenes. If you don't have enough clientele, you are the one who has to do something to change that. Putting yourself out there, living through the trials of people coming and going, finding a stable sense of security during slow times, and building a strong-enough practice that you do not have slow times—this all takes years of labor.

While this shadow-why can exist for a person from any walk of life, it is important to note that comparing your practice to that of someone with more societal privilege is unkind to yourself. Many people gain success or appear to gain success through privileges that may not be overt. While the privileges that come with whiteness can be more visible, many of them are not; and privileges associated with class access can be even less so. It is easy to compare one's self to others and feel inferior; however, don't forget that surviving in a capitalist landscape is anything but a level playing field. For example, building a practice requires that you can financially support yourself while you don't have any clientele. Some people do that by working a second job, which can make it difficult to give enough attention to their fledgling practice. Others have the wealth privilege to not work while their practice is getting off the ground. Bring compassion to yourself and the circumstances you live in. Compassion includes not comparing yourself to others.

Fantasizing about the easeful success story is a method of using entitlement as a defense against grief and shame. It is often associated with being wounded or traumatized as a child and is an attachment to innocence and being parented or being the innocent child. When we survive trauma and wounding as children (from our families or society), we suffer a loss of innocence. The reality is that the trauma or wounding happened, and that nothing will ever make it not have happened. In this sense, entitlement can be a defense against accepting reality. I believe that humans are capable of immense healing, but you will always be a person who had that experience. If this scenario resonates with you: the reality is that you really didn't have enough as a child, and you will actually have to work hard to get enough now. The reality is that people hurt you as a child, and there will be many more people on your path who will remind you of that pain. There is no magical parent who is going to come in and build your practice for you. None of your colleagues will revere you enough to heal the ways that you were not delighted in or seen as a child. None of the people you will work with are going to love you enough to repair the ways you may not have been loved enough in other relationships—and that is a disservice to their healing if you are unconsciously making this request. As painful as it is, whatever you lost through trauma and wounding will need to be lovingly grieved.

Being new at something can elicit shame. If you set out to build a healing practice, you will invariably have times when you do not have a thriving practice. Weathering those times with grace requires a certain level of self-love and self-confidence that many of us struggle to generate so early in our paths. At times, entitlement is a welcomed defense against this shame. It can be compelling to look out at the world and say, "I should have more and it is not my fault that I don't!" Underneath that statement might be other thoughts, such as: "Why am I struggling so much?" "Is there something wrong with me?" "Am I any good at this profession?" These are more tender and vulnerable questions. The answer might be that something outside of you is part of the problem: perhaps you work in a community that is not familiar with the type of healing you offer. Or the answer might be that something inside of you does need to change: it is possible that you will need more skills than you currently have before your practice thrives. While the entitlement may temporarily blow off some steam, the exploration of the more vulnerable questions is what cultivates a state of empowerment so that you can take action wherever possible.

If you need to be revered all the time, you will be unable to be your true healer self because you will be trapped by criticism and/or lack of attention from others. If you live in the fantasy that your practice should grow without working very hard, you will always be disappointed at how little it is growing, and you will feel powerless to change it. Rather than letting entitlement, rejection of grief, shame, or an excessive need for reverence unconsciously run your practice, consider building a relationship with it. You can speak to these parts directly and lovingly. You can ask what they need and you can comfort them. You can also compassionately name them when they appear: "There you are again, Entitlement." "There you are again, Shame." "There you are again, kid-who-needs-more-witnessing." Let yourself be curious about these emotional needs and tend to them so that you don't try to tend to them through your practice.

Wanting Love

We started to touch on this in the case of wanting to be revered, but let's dive deeper, because this is a very common shadow-why for healers and it is not always coupled with entitlement or a need for reverence. First, I want to say: it is okay to want and need love. You deserve love, and you are a human being so you need it for your survival. However, wanting to be loved in tandem with *being unwilling to be disliked* presents some complications. Being a skilled healer can result in being a bit idealized by the people you have helped. Do I love my therapist? Yes. Has she helped to steward me through the most painful parts of my healing process? Yes. Do I wonder how she is such a magical person and completely idealize her? Sometimes. That type of power and idealization can be alluring, especially if you struggle with your own self-esteem and self-love. However, as a healer, your job is not to be liked; it is to be honest. Sometimes people come to you because they are not behaving well and are hurting themselves or others. Or perhaps they engage in a lifestyle that contributes to chronic pain or other physical ailments you are treating. If you were working with someone who was hitting their spouse, would you avoid honest conversation about that in order to be liked? Would you avoid confronting lifestyle choices that contribute to physical illness? Very skilled healers are willing to risk being disliked in order to help people heal. Sometimes we point out patterns of behavior that people do not like about themselves, and they can be prickly in response to being seen to that degree.

In the case of healers who work in the psychological realm, it may be that someone you work with actually needs to be allowed to dislike you as part of their healing. Many people are angry at their primary caregivers or other loved ones and have not had the space to be angry while still being cared for and accepted. Sometimes this dynamic is constellated in service of deeper healing. However, in order to allow for this, you will need to tolerate someone not liking you and remain curious about their dislike, rather than reject it.

Looking back to my example of the time when I was overidentified with being a generous caregiver, let's recall: *I didn't want to be disliked by my peers.* My need to be nonthreatening and loved by my peers informed how I set my fees, which contributed to substantial financial stress. Making choices about your practice or life path in order to be loved by others sets you up to live a life that isn't your own. Many of these choices are based on the fantasy of what you think others will feel about you, not what they actually feel. This can impact every aspect of your practice and very negatively impact the healing work you do with others. It also doesn't work because you cannot please everyone and you cannot predict how others will feel about your choices (though you can exhaust yourself trying).

A classic example of this can be seen in how healers build their websites. If you are a person who wants to be loved, liked, or respected by your peers, you may find yourself writing content for your website that is directed toward them. You may agonize over what others will think of what you have written. Does it sound smart enough, did you read enough theory in grad school or will everyone know you definitely skipped a few articles, do you sound caring enough? And on and on. Who is your website for? It is for people who will potentially work with you. It is for your peers only in the sense that you want them to feel comfortable sharing your website for referrals. Healers tend to write websites full of jargon that most people don't have a reference for, except other healers. Waxing poetic on "embodiment" and the "holding environment" and your grasp of "holistic healing" may sound good to peers, but it doesn't share your personality or your underlying "why" for someone to connect with.

Having a personality means that you are not a neutral being. There will always be people who like you and people who don't. People who hide their personalities are often harder to connect to, and this creates big problems for healers (because most of our livelihoods depend on making meaningful connections). Ultimately, the question is: do you love yourself? Learning to love all parts of you—the altruistic parts and the entitled, needy, ashamed, or childish parts—creates an environment for your more-unconscious wounds to be tended to consciously. Engaging these parts of yourself sets you free from needing your peers and clients to fill your wounds with their love. Healers, and all care workers, also need to be embedded in loving, satisfying relationships outside of our work in order to sustain such an intense level of giving.

Wanting to Be Seen as Good or Sane

A close cousin to wanting to be loved is wanting to be seen as good or sane. The well-regarded psychoanalyst Ronald Fairbairn once said, "it is better to be a sinner in a world ruled by God than to live in a world ruled by the Devil."[4] If you have severe childhood trauma, or you grew up in a particularly critical household, or you have been systematically treated as mentally unwell by society, this shadow-why might be familiar. It is reasonable to want to feel sane and good. You should never have been treated any other way as a child or an adult. To be made to feel that one is bad or wrong at a core level is a form of abuse and degradation of one's inherent value. Pervasive feelings of intense shame and a perception that one is a "bad person" or "crazy" often originate from being heavily projected onto as children or suffering other forms of abuse. As a child living in an abusive environment, it would be entirely too destabilizing to see one's self as an innocent victim to an abusive caregiver or loved one. To stay present to the reality that you are powerless in "hell" is intolerable. In an effort to defend against such a reality, children often see themselves as the problem, thus allowing the "badness" to be inside of them and not in their environment, which subsequently allows them to work to make themselves better, as though they could someday control how bad things are by controlling how bad they are. This trauma narrative may sound familiar to you from Christian supremacy and other religious environments that purport that you are a sinner by nature who must spend your life in a form of debt redeemable only by being good and proving your worthiness in order to eventually be accepted (into heaven). Additionally, there may have been times in your life when you operated more from your wounds than from your highest self, and you may have regrets about those times, or feel ashamed of your behaviors.

One quick and dirty way to see yourself as "better" or "sane" is to surround yourself with people who you deem are worse off than you. You are no longer the one with the pain and chaos inside; it is the people you work with. You are no longer the one who needs to "get their life together"; it is the people you work with. You are not an unstable person who struggles with wildly vacillating self-esteem and acting out your pain, because you are a healer and healers do not do things like that!

Most of what we project onto other people are things that we are not yet ready to face in ourselves. As a healer, you are signing up for a lifetime of exploring everything you do not like about yourself and learning to love it, or at minimum accept it.

The people you work with are vulnerable, especially if they are idealizing you or hoping that you are the one who can truly help them heal. They need to be accurately understood in the severity of their issues, but they do not need to be judged or projected onto. Some people who come to us are very unwell. These people are some of the most vulnerable to projections. If people you work with or others in your life describe feeling degraded, criticized, or judged by you—take special note of this feedback, as it may be pointing to this dynamic. Any type of healing practitioner can engage in psychological projections, even if you are a practitioner who does not specifically work in a psychological manner (i.e., healers working with physical ailments). Again, the antidote to projecting onto others is to explore and name these issues in yourself. The more conscious they become, the less harm they will cause in your practice.

Wanting to Heal Your Parents or Primary Caregivers

Oftentimes children who grow up in homes with caregivers who are not well fantasize or hope that their caregiver(s) will recover or heal; for example, the child who wishes their parent would stop drinking and finally show them the attention they desperately need. Healers can sometimes bring this longing into their practice and become overly invested in their client's healing. That might sound strange, because of course you are invested in their healing. What does it even mean to be "overly invested"? Sometimes we work with people who do not heal, or they heal in very small steps, or they struggle to stick with the work and end the healing relationship before healing can happen. This is just a fact of life and part of their process. Being overly invested happens when you expect them to heal in ways that *you determine* or at a pace that *you determine,* regardless of the level of disturbance they are reporting or what they have actually said they want. Some people are struggling in ways that may mean, for example, that they long to be sober, but that they are not going to be. Or that they need to change their diet for a medical condition, and will not do it. If you find yourself becoming triggered, controlling, or having the same level of disappointment toward your clients that you have toward your parents, you are probably overinvested. It is important to remember that these are not people you rely on the way you relied on your primary caregivers as a child. They are allowed to use substances or never leave the abusive partner for as long as that is what they choose. Of course, if that is too painful for you to work with, you don't have to specialize in people who remind you of your parents. However, often people do specialize in people with similar issues as their parents, in an attempt to heal the part of them that really needed a parent who was willing to change. This is another scenario that ends up being a defense against grief. If only the parent (or the client you are projecting onto) would heal, then you wouldn't have to grieve. However, the truth is: you will have to grieve regardless of anyone else's healing progress. What you lived through was real. And no one's healing is going to erase the past.

* * *

Uncovering your shadow-why is not to shame or blame you; it isn't to beat yourself up and instigate a spiral into your own personal hell. It is to get curious about parts of you that need and deserve attention, so that you can offer incredible healing work without these parts interfering. Ultimately, knowing these parts of yourself will also create more capacity to see and compassionately engage with them in the people you work with.

A simple way to find out about some of what you project onto other people is to notice what you really do not like about others. People often say that what you don't like in someone else is a reflection of what you do not like in yourself. That is not always true. Sometimes we don't like a person or someone's actions, and it has nothing to do with our disowned material. But what really tips me off that the dislike is about disowned material is when

I or someone else complains at length about another person's behavior, or when it seems that I or they cannot stop thinking about it. And it is most likely a projection if that behavior isn't even impacting the person who is complaining about it. So if you are stumped on where to start, just think about qualities you cannot stand in other people, then take a look in the mirror.

3.1 *Reflection*

1. What did you feel while you read this chapter?

2. What memories, if any, emerged?

3. What sensations did you feel in your body while you read this chapter? The largest clusters of your nervous system are in your head, your heart/chest, and your belly. You can do the body scan exercise from chapter 1; however, a quick alternative is to go right to your breath, your heart/chest, and your belly and notice what is happening there.

3.2 *Writing*

1. What thoughts or feelings emerged as you read this chapter? Start writing and let yourself be truthful (while also being kind to yourself).

2. When you imagine yourself as a healer, what do you fantasize it could be like?

3. Are there parts of you that never feel complete or that get activated in times of stress?

4. When you fantasize about who you want to be as a healer, what difficult emotions does this fantasy help to repair?

5. How can you say hello to these emotions and get to know them better? What would help to build a conscious relationship to them?

6. What practices do you have that let you know you love yourself?

7. Do you need to pursue more healing around these issues; and if so, what will that look like?

3.3 *Ritual Conversation*

Once you get clear on some of your shadow-whys, choose one to work with more in depth. Invite your chosen shadow-why to sit down for a cup of tea and get into a conversation. You could actually set up a ritual tea space or just imagine this space in your mind. Either way, make it intentional space and give yourself the time to see where the conversation takes you. If you don't know where to start, ask this part of yourself to tell you more about its life, the same as you might when meeting any new person. More involved questions could include: What does the shadow-why need? What beliefs does the shadow-why hold about the world and about you? Anytime that you are hosting a guest, you thank the guest for coming and make sure that the guest is comfortable—host this guest as you would host any important guest.

Who Are You Here to Work With?

I f you are in this work for the long haul, you need to develop your practice around who you are. By tailoring your practice around your personality and purpose you allow yourself to do your best work and prevent burnout. Burning out happens when we do not take care of ourselves, and neglecting your higher purpose or calling falls into that category. To sustain the level of giving required in being a healing practitioner, you will need to be inspired and fed by this work.

Many practitioners overfocus on money, feeling that if they are paid "enough" they can work with anyone. I once heard a struggling clinician say they wanted to "specialize in rich people" because they were so frustrated by not making enough income. While I support you to be financially stable and that is an important part of the sustainability of your practice, you are not compensated for your work solely with money. Your work also fulfills a sense of purpose and gives your life meaning, which no amount of money can replace. Earning money is a necessary evil in a capitalist system, but it is not a life goal. This perspective is also harmful to your clients and constellates a wound that many owning-class people struggle with: questioning if anyone actually loves them or wants a real relationship with them, outside of money.

We all have limitations and that includes limits on who we can help and who we cannot. It is a rough go to learn where these limits lie, as these lessons usually come in the form of failures and frustrations. Over time, it is essential to seek clarity and ask yourself: who am I here to work with?

Creating healing relationships is as complex as creating friendships or romantic relationships. You wouldn't partner with just anyone, you wouldn't be friends with just anyone, and you shouldn't accompany someone on their healing journey just because they contacted you. They choose you, but you also need to choose them. If you have a history of your consent being violated or of feeling trapped in unfulfilling or abusive relationships, this lesson is essential to understand. Healers can easily be caught in enactments of their own trauma, and feeling that you have no right to consent to a relationship does not create a healing container for good work to happen. Even if most people who contact you will be a good fit, there always needs to be room to say "no."

While you need to be discerning in whom you work with, I want to stress that I am not suggesting denying access to healing based on prejudice, stereotypes, ableism, racism, or any other form of systemic oppression. Capitalism is a global, cultural structure that functions by devaluing and vilifying some (this devaluing then justifies paying them less and exploiting them) while overvaluing and idealizing others (this overvaluing then justifies paying them more at the expense of exploitation of others). No one is immune to the beliefs underlying capitalism. In a 2016 study seeking to investigate differences in access to care between white and Black people and middle-class and working-class people, it was found that potential psychotherapy clients who were middle class were offered appointments with therapists almost three times more than their working-class counterparts. Race and gender were also factors in whether or not someone was offered care.[5] The people in this study are healing practitioners. They have committed their lives to supporting others to heal from wounding, and yet they are participating in the creation of more of it.

Despite our best intentions, none of us is immune to the ideas we were socialized with as part of our culture. Despite what society teaches us, when we talk about working with clients who are a "great fit," that is not a code phrase for working with wealthy people, able-bodied people, white people, or any other idealized, overly privileged group. Most people exist at some intersection of privilege and oppression and therefore each of us needs to work at undoing the oppressive structures that exist in our minds and souls. Without that undoing, we will just unconsciously perpetuate oppression, even in the realm of healing.

Alternatively, working with someone who is more oppressed than you, just to make yourself feel less guilty about your privilege, is also not an answer. If you are an owning-class person and you feel guilty about that and decide to take on some working-class clients to feel less guilty, that is not an offering. That is using your clients to process your own guilt. We also need to work with people we are knowledgeable about. That doesn't mean that you cannot work with someone who is different from you, but it does mean that you need to educate yourself about whom you are working with. Some of this education comes directly from the people you are working with, but much of it comes from your own actions of reading and listening to what others have offered about specific populations and life experiences. If you are working with someone who has a traumatic immigration story and you do not have relatable life experience, you don't need to press them to educate you. Many memoirs, media articles, songs, and other forms of expression are available to learn about immigration trauma.

While I support efforts to build cross-cultural working skills that allow for excellent care within dynamics of sociocultural power differentials, at times these attempts neglect to ask the question: why are there so few healers available with marginalized identities? For example, transgender people often do not get the choice to work with a transgender provider, because the only options may be cisgender providers. There are many aspects of oppression that limit who has the ability to pursue the role of healership; however, one aspect that we as healers have the power to change is the institutions we learn in. As reported by many of my peers, my graduate school was quite hostile toward people of color. A lot of becoming a healer in any realm is about surviving the institutions that you actually have to learn in. People who have power within our institutions need to be thinking critically about how to make educational resources accessible and supportive to all bodies and all incomes. Accessibility is a lot more than just offering someone massive financial debt and a tokenizing learning environment.

What I want to stress is that if you don't consciously think through these beliefs and work to transform them, you will likely unconsciously operate in a way that further perpetuates oppression. Even if you are a very oppressed person, you are still capable of perpetuating more oppression onto others. Remember my colleague who said, "I want to specialize in rich people." That came from a very vulnerable place; that colleague was not making enough money to survive. However, specializing in "rich people" means that you are committed to excluding poor people, working-class people, and even middle-class people from your healing practice. That perpetuates oppression. Many people don't outright say they specialize in rich people, but they build their business models in such a way that they essentially do. When you specialize in rich people, that means you are mostly going to be working with white people, able-bodied people, cisgender people, highly educated people, etc.—you get where I am going with this. I want to support you to think about who you are, actually here, on this earth, in this moment, to work with. That means getting outside of your social conditioning, rejecting a scarcity model, and building a practice that can sustain the type of work you are meant to do. If you are in private practice and you are meant to work with a population that cannot financially sustain you, you can diversify your offerings, work with an ample sliding scale, take on people with a variety of incomes to supplement your work, and you can also consider partnering with organizations and applying for grants. The reality is that someone from any walk of life could be a good fit for you, and someone who seems just like you could be terrible. Assessing the right fit is complex.

While considering the identities of the people you work with is important, you can also consider the qualities of the people you work best with. I know for myself anxiety is more my flow than depression. I can roll with a full-blown panic attack better than a session of barely any speaking. That doesn't mean I don't work with people who get depressed, but it does mean that more of my practice is people who tend toward anxiety. Before we dive too deep into the qualities of who you work with, let's break down some important aspects of what supports effective healing.

You need two things to make a healing relationship work: competence and chemistry. First, let's explore competence. Great practitioners know their limits. There are some issues that you actually need to know a lot about in order to work with them. As you develop your craft and get some years under your belt, this will become more clear. If someone calls you up and wants to work on issues you know nothing about, you will need to ask yourself a few questions: What are you willing to learn in order to work with this person? Is the issue something that truly requires a specialist? Is there a lack of services in your area that would ethically necessitate flexibility around competence?

Sometimes life experience and training can be translated to work with issues that are newer to you, and sometimes they cannot. If you are a breathworker and someone comes to you and wants support around the death of a friend, and you have never had a friend die or supported anyone who has had a friend die, but you have had a parent die, that might be enough for you to say "yes" to supporting them through the grief process. However, if you are an acupuncturist specializing in physical pain relief, and someone comes to you with severe infertility issues, you will have to assess if it is ethical to work with this person. If you work in a rural setting where you are the only acupuncturist for 150 miles, then perhaps you would let them know your scope of competence, but consider working with them and seek consultation to ensure the best possible care.

When it comes to something truly requiring a specialist, I like to consider how much harm is possible. If the worst harm is that your work is not very effective and you have been transparent about your limitations, but plan to work together for other reasons (rural area, perhaps you have another specialty that does connect with them, etc.), that might be fine. However, if not being specialized can cause significant harm, that is an issue, and working together potentially becomes unethical. As a person who works in the very specialized field of sexual trauma, I come up against these issues a lot.

Many people don't see sexual trauma as a specialized issue but carry the perspective that any therapist, regardless of training, can work with this type of trauma. Yet, I can't tell you how many people I have worked with who saw a therapist before me who told the client what they experienced "wasn't rape." Rule number one in working with sexual trauma: the therapist's job is not to give an opinion on if the trauma actually occurred. However, if most of your knowledge about sexual trauma comes through reading about it in the news and hearing about it in the media, you might think that is an appropriate treatment of it, because that is exactly what happens in the public discourse: not believing the survivor. Those therapists may have felt that they really helped their clients by relieving them of the narrative that they were raped, when in fact they caused an immense amount of pain. To finally work up the courage to seek help and then be told what you experienced wasn't real—this is an injury. If you aren't familiar with a highly specific issue, you can cause lasting harm by working with someone of that population.

Assessing for scope of competence is a skill and you will develop it more with time. If someone is not within your scope of competence, all you need to do is let them know this and be sure to make a referral to someone you think could be a good fit.

Next up: chemistry. What is healing chemistry? Healing chemistry is the alchemical interaction between two or more people that can result in integration, growth, and wholeness. As with all things, at the base level you've got three options as an outcome of an attempt at healing: things can get better, get worse, or stay the same. Of course, complexity exists in all areas of life, and while one thing gets better it is possible for another thing to get worse; but in the realm of healing, really good healing relationships should not include dramatic or notable injury at the expense of healing. When there is good chemistry in a healing relationship the work flows. That doesn't mean that it is always easy, but that there is a functional working relationship. It should allow you to grow, to be met, and to feel on your path. A shadow in the realm of healing is to think that healing practitioners should give selflessly, with no needs in the relationship. Selfless giving is draining. There is a difference between *using* the people you work with versus *receiving* from the exchange.

Making your entire practice a strong fit with your personality and path allows you to do your best work, feel motivated, and look forward to continuing on in your career. And *that* helps the people you work with. It is okay to feel tired after work, or to feel exhausted if you had a big week; but if you are working with people who make you feel completely drained, and it is not because you didn't get enough sleep the night before, it is important to think about the long-term impact of having several healing relationships like this. As a healing practitioner, you will do your best work when you are fed. You cannot offer something to people when you are entirely depleted and unhappy. You need to be living life in a way that is in integrity with your own healing in order to offer people your services.

For many healing practitioners the very notion that you could build a practice like this is radical. There is so much scarcity mentality in the realm of business-building and healing that promotes the idea that you can never say "no" to a potential client. However, finding the courage to say "no" is the gift of honesty. It is a gift to them and a gift to you. It also helps you stay in integrity—these people are not your paycheck. Yes, they pay you, but if you cannot help them or don't truly want to work with them, it is your duty to say "no" to them. This allows them to seek out the person they will do stronger work with, and it allows you to keep space open for the person who is eventually coming your way. You don't know when someone contacts you what your role is in their life. It might be as a matchmaker. Some people come to you just so you can send them to someone else.

How will you answer the question: who am I here to work with? Discerning who you work best with requires experience, reflection, and trust in yourself. You may already know who you work best with, but if you don't listen to that knowing, you are right back at the beginning. The answer to this question may be something you have known from the outset of your process or something you are still quite unclear on. Personally, who I am meant to work with changes and becomes more refined over the years. Working with a wide swath of people at the beginning of my career was helpful in my own discernment. If you are at the beginning of your practice or even just at the start of contemplating stepping onto this path, just explore. Work with many types of people and be observant about your experiences with them. The only rule you must always follow is: do not harm. If you think you are harming to someone, it is not appropriate to explore working with them. Though if you are early in your path, note that there is a difference between causing harm and making mistakes or being clumsy with your skills. Learning necessitates making mistakes.

The next step in discerning is to look at what you already know, which I suggest doing from both a thinking place and an embodied place. The body is truly the final say in most matters, so now is always the time to listen to it. Take some time to think about the people you work with now; and if you don't have current clients, you can think about past clients or people you have helped in nonworking environments, such as friends and community members. Really consider who you loved working with and who you did not. Get out a piece of paper and start writing. Think of the people you loved working with—what kind of people are they? What do they bring out in you? How do they make you feel? What is the quality of connection? Perhaps you like working with people who are shy and slow to open up; maybe you enjoy the long process of watching someone slowly unfold. Perhaps you can be shy and easily overwhelmed, and perhaps you like working with others who really take it slow. Or maybe you enjoy working with people who have big personalities and are talkative and quick to connect. Whatever it is, write it down. Get clear on it. And get clear on how they make you feel. Do you feel useful? As though your work has meaning? Do you feel moved? Do you feel at ease? Do you feel that you are doing your best work? Think back to your "why" and your "shadow-why." These inquiries can be a guide to this next step of discernment. Perhaps part of *why* you do this work is tied in with *who* you are meant to serve.

Now let's turn to people you did not work well with. What qualities are difficult for you? These qualities could be just a bad alchemical reaction with your personality, or it could be due to your own personal wounding or trauma. If you are a quiet person who is drained by loud, talkative interactions, you will probably not fare well having an entire practice of people like this. If you grew up in a family that interrupts, jumps back and forth in conversations, and is generally excitable, it might feel very confining for you to work with people who need a lot of quiet and zero interrupting.

Relating to your personal trauma, there are places we grow an ability to work with things that trigger us and then places we just accept a limit around. For example, if you are an entheogenic or psychedelic medicine guide and had an alcoholic caregiver, and find that you cannot stay present working with someone who is struggling with alcohol and also has children, you have to decide if you are going to do the personal work required to heal yourself enough that you can remain present to your medicine and be able to offer it with compassion in a situation like this. I encourage you to push yourself, while also accepting your limits. You are not required to be continually re-traumatized in your work, and you may decide that this is not who you are meant to work with. However, if you decide to do the healing required to show up for people who remind you of your trauma, you also offer incredible insight into situations you have lived through. While that parent struggling with alcohol talks about how they think their kids don't love them, you will have the insight that perhaps their children love them fiercely but are terrified to be close to someone who abandons them. That is wisdom.

Another way you can learn about who you are not meant to work with is to notice: which of your worst qualities come out when you are working with someone who is not a good fit? Many healing practitioners report feeling unempathetic, judgmental, or impatient when working with a less-than-optimal fit. It's not a good look and it doesn't feel stellar to think about, but it is honest and important to note. The more that you know how you behave when the relationship isn't working, the more able you will be to save your clients from yourself and refer out before the relationship is harming.

I mentioned exploring this question from an embodied place. While thinking is very useful, your body reflects many of your unconscious thoughts and can sometimes tell you more than you may be aware of in your conscious mind. When I talk about embodiment with trauma survivors, they often say, "But Laura, my body feels so many ways and I cannot tell if I am triggered or if I am really picking up on something in the moment." If you are consistently triggered with a client and it is not resolving by addressing it in your own healing, you should not work with them. You cannot do good work if you are activated beyond the ability to think, feel, and sense your body. So a very strong internal "no" response will likely just mean "no" regardless of whether it is related to the person or to your own trauma.

When you have trauma or wounding that either has made you numb (unable to feel much in your body) or has rendered you overly responsive (feeling flooded with internal sensations), it can seem impossible to determine what you are actually feeling, and many people abandon the body as a source of information and rely primarily on thinking. Learning to listen to your body is like learning a language. It takes time to understand its communications. With ample practice you can start to determine the difference between the sensation of nontraumatic stress and the sensation of being triggered around traumatic material. Often when I ask people to feel into their bodies, they close their eyes for five seconds and then open them and continue chattering away. It takes more than five seconds. Think about when you watch a movie or read a book: how much time is dedicated to learning about the characters—you are learning about yourself and *you will need time* to know yourself more intimately. Being embodied and listening to yourself at that level is a life's work. If you don't already have an embodiment practice, you can start today. It is very simple: you just need to pay attention to the sensations in your body and stay curious about them. If that is too painful to do, as it often is for people with substantial trauma or wounding, you can start by only paying attention to your breathing. What really makes an embodiment practice work is repetition. If you spend ten minutes or more per day for a year having an intimate conversation with yourself through listening to your own body, you will have developed much more self-intimacy and knowing. That self-knowledge will ultimately assist you in the big path-defining choices about who you will offer your work to.

======= EXERCISES AND EXPERIENTIALS =======

CHAPTER 4

4.1 *Reflection*

1. What did you feel while you read this chapter?

2. What memories, if any, emerged?

3. What sensations did you feel in your body while you read this chapter?

4.2 *Writing*

1. Think of people you feel a great chemistry working with. What types of qualities do they have?

2. What do they bring out in you?

3. What is the quality of connection?

4. How do you end up feeling when you work with someone you have great healing chemistry with?

5. Now let's turn to people you do not work well with. What qualities are difficult for you in the people you serve?

6. Which of your worst qualities come out when you are working with someone who is not a good fit?

7. What are the signs that something is not working?

8. How do you feel when you work with someone who is not a good fit for you?

4.3 *Body Scan*

Using the same body scan from chapter 1 (or do a shorter version by focusing on your breath, your heart/chest, and your belly), bring to mind someone or some qualities that are a great fit for you. Notice the sensorial cues that let you know this person or these qualities are a good fit. Do you feel warm? Do you feel soft? Do you feel enlivened? When you are done with exploring what a good fit feels like, bring to mind someone or some qualities that are ill fitting for you. Notice the sensorial cues that let you know something is not working well. Do you feel afraid? Do you feel dull? Do you feel judgmental? Continue to build awareness of similar sensorial cues you receive in daily life. It is important to know what the signs are and listen to them.

4.4 Research

As stated in the chapter, knowing what is a good fit or a bad fit for you is not intended to be an avenue to uphold oppression or stereotypes. What work have you done to explore your implicit bias or the unconscious ways you hold oppressive narratives? If this is something you have never thought about previously, or have never given much time to, consider taking a training or seeking out other resources (books, films, lectures) to learn about how privilege and oppression play out interpersonally and systemically. In addition to understanding *what* is happening, consider seeking guidance on *how* to interrupt and not perpetuate harmful dynamics.

Creating a Niche, or
Writing Your Prayer

The progression of these chapters is guiding you to hone more and more of who you are as a healing practitioner and what your intentions are in this work. Beyond understanding *who* you are going to work with is understanding the *niche* you will work in.

What is a niche? A niche is the area of specialty that you work in. It can be tempting not to build a niche, because you may be thinking: *If I get too specialized, people will not contact me because I don't put out the message that I work with them.* However, the problem with that line of thinking is that if you get too broad, people will also not contact you, because you aren't specialized enough. If you work in a small town where the market isn't saturated with what you do, and you are, say, one of the only acupuncturists they have to choose from, you may not be forced to find as much of a niche. However, if you work in a large, saturated area where there are many acupuncturists to choose from, you will need a niche. When someone looks on your website and sees that you specifically work with fertility issues and they have fertility issues, they are more likely to call you than if it just says you are an acupuncturist who works with everyone. If you work in a region that is not saturated, but you do work remotely, let's say you are a tarot reader who uses technology to connect with clients at a distance, then you definitely work in a saturated location (the entire world) and having a niche is essential. Additionally, thinking a niche will scare potential clients away comes from a scarcity model. Don't plan to fail; plan to succeed. Defining your niche is a part of walking your path, rather than walking the one you think is more popular, more acceptable, or more appealing to others.

We will get back to the logistical and concrete reasons why you need to build a niche, but before that, let's explore the spiritual significance of having a niche.

What is a prayer? For many people, prayer is essentially considered talking to "God." And for many people, "God" is considered a distinct divine being. I am using the term "prayer" to mean the sacred intention you want to communicate to the world, to humanity, to spirit. This frame does not require you to adhere to a specific religion or believe in specific gods, and you can adapt and shift my perspective until it resonates with yours. This is not dogma; it is an invitation to view your offerings through a spiritual lens.

To this point we have covered a lot about intention and purpose; your niche is the next step in bringing all of that together. It is the expressed vision of all the things we have covered in the preceding chapters. It is the medicine you bring to the world, the people you bring it to, and the outcome you offer. It is imbued with your underlying purpose—the reason "why" you do this work. As an example, consider someone who has decided to become a healing voice instructor. Perhaps this person started out as a vocalist, but had an innate sense that something about song, sound, and the use of one's body had helped them and could help others. Perhaps singing helped them through a time of tremendous grief. As they soul-search and identify what they want to offer, they decide that they want to lead singing groups for people who have lost a loved one to suicide and that they are available to work with groups of people who share community when there has been a community loss. This is a prayer in the making. This healer is offering the hope of embodied growth and transformation to those who have suffered the pain of loss, through connection to one of the instruments of their physical being: voice.

Your niche is your prayer. You need one to stay connected to the spiritual meaning of your life's work. Practically speaking, you need a niche in order to communicate to the people you will work with and to the people who will refer clients to you. Remember, prayer is talking *to* something or someone. Once you have identified your niche or prayer, you will need to share it with the world, which we will cover in a later chapter.

Over time, having a niche helps to increase your skill set. Let's take the healing voice instructor as an example. When this person first starts practicing, they are going to operate with the knowledge of how they healed their own wounds with song. That is powerful, but it is a fairly small subset of humanity (meaning precisely one person). However, through years of working with hundreds of grieving people, they will learn so much more about how to support people who are grieving. Each person they work with is offering a unique view into the human spirit. The people we work with are our teachers and increase our skill in working with others. One of the best forms of marketing is being good at your job. You could do a lot of intake sessions, but you have to be good at what you do to sustain a practice. Having a niche supports you to do your best work.

As I said earlier, one of the most common things I hear in response to creating a niche is: "If I get too specialized, people will not contact me because I don't put out the message that I work with them." When someone is lost, confused, or hurting and needs support, they want to work with someone who is confident and clear. Confident doesn't mean being arrogant, inauthentic, or falsely representing one's skills. It means knowing your true capacity, within your limitations. Clarity does not mean that your practice is narrow and inflexible, or that you are unable to work with someone adjacent to your niche. It means that you know what you offer, and you are making a particular space to meet the particular needs of the people you work with. Having a prayer, committing to a niche—this communicates a level of confidence and direction that helps people feel contained and safe. People will come to you for all sorts of reasons. It could be that something you specialize in is not exactly their pain, but perhaps it is the pain of someone close to them. For example, you could specialize in immigration stress, and someone might come to you because that is the stress their parents or grandparents endured, and they want to know that you understand that aspect of their lineage. Or perhaps you specialize in working with queer people, and someone comes to you not because they are a queer person, but because their parents are queer and they feel most comfortable in queer-friendly environments.

Your colleagues are an important part of sustaining your practice, because they are a part of your prayer getting out to the world. As healing practitioners, we need to actively make referrals. A referral is when you give someone who needs help the name of a practitioner you suggest working with. Your colleagues need to know what your prayer is; they need a strong sense of your niche. The more confident and clear you are about what your purpose is, the more others will understand it and feel comfortable referring to you.

When you formulate a niche, remember that your own needs must be met for you to sustain yourself. You may feel called to work with severe trauma or hard-to-treat medical symptoms; but if that is the case, you will need to think critically about how you are going to weather the intensity that comes with that work so that you do not burn out. It is rare that someone can handle an entire caseload of severe trauma, or patients who are constantly navigating uncertainty around their health. You may find that you are more able to do this in a group practice, where you feel the support of colleagues. Or that you want to balance your niche out. For example, balancing out work with survivors of intimate partner violence, with people seeking spiritual development, or working with chronic pain, balanced with nutritional coaching. Whatever your niche is will impact you, and that is okay, but you will need to pay close attention to *how* it impacts you and nourish yourself enough to show up to the work.

For some of us, we choose a niche that is stigmatized, and there can be some unique fears and repercussions for doing that. For example, I specialize in working with sex workers. Many people have big feelings about sex work, and I have received a small amount of harsh feedback because of it. Work related to race, religion, sexual orientation, gender identity, abortions, BDSM, and many other contentious issues may result in some level of aggression or judgment from others. That can include anything from verbal harassment to physical harm to someone choosing not to work with you because of the populations you serve. It is important to think about your personal safety as well as what you are meant to do in your life. While there may be small or large risks based on the work you do, do not underestimate the harm that comes from hiding and ignoring your purpose. If you are very worried about this, you can look to what other practitioners have done to keep themselves safe.

Remember that your niche can change. At minimum it will deepen and evolve, but it can also make a dramatic transition. Human beings are dynamic, and your spiritual path may look very different in ten years. Defining your niche is a serious task, but all you need to do is start where you are at now. You don't need to bog yourself down with a commitment to eternity; you get to change.

CHAPTER 5

5.1 *Writing*

1. What fears do you have about honing your craft even further and defining a niche?

2. What hopes or excitements do you have about defining a niche? How do you see it being useful?

3. Begin to define your niche through writing: write the prayer that you have for what type of issues you will be specializing in and the healing and growth you will be offering others. How would you describe this? Remember, your niche can grow over time; just give it your best shot and describe what this is to you right now.

4. If you are not sure about your niche, make a list of topics that interest you. After you feel finished with that list, make another list of experiences that might help you get more clear on which of these pertain to your true calling. These could be experiences such as volunteering with a certain population, working with a particular healer, taking a training, reading a book, doing a ritual, etc.

5.2 *Ritual*

After you have written your niche prayer, set aside some uninterrupted time in a space conducive to mindfulness. If you have an existing ritual practice or altar, you are welcome to add to this ritual in whatever way makes sense to you. Start by cleaning the space you will be in. Next, place your prayer next to you so you can easily access it. To begin, take an action that indicates the ritual is starting—this could be lighting a candle, saying a prayer, singing a song, calling on the support and protection of loved ones, etc. Now take some time to be still, and turn your attention inward to your breath. Notice how you are feeling internally; if you feel particularly rushed or activated, now may not be the time for this ritual. If you are feeling present and fairly calm, turn your attention to the prayer next to you. With full presence, read the prayer to yourself. Now sit with openness and listen—what does your body tell you about this prayer? Was every part of it accurate? Was there anything that needed to change to be more aligned with you? If you have a practice of connecting to your ancestors, spirits, or other entities—invite guidance from them and tune into your body and the ways that you receive information from them. When you feel complete, mark the end of the ritual with thanks and any action that helps you close it—a prayer, a song, blowing out the candle. If there were things that needed to change about your prayer, rewrite it and keep dropping in to assess as you go.

5.3 *Play*

If you have come to this point in the book and you are feeling pretty lost about answering these questions: play. Don't labor at it. Go forth in the world and play, but play with awareness. Spend time with friends, make new friends, go dancing, get in contact with your aliveness and see where that takes you. Play is how we learn about ourselves and our interests. If you haven't played enough or had enough experience in life, it can be hard to define yourself. You might love dance, but you don't know yet because you have never tried it. People can get way too serious when it comes to healing and seeking out a life path. Lose yourself in the fun, forget what you are trying to achieve, and be with the joy of life.

REVIEW AND SHIFTING FOCUS

All of the preceding chapters are leading you toward a more cohesive understanding of yourself in relationship to your path. Just as many organizations have a mission statement, you have intentions. Living a fulfilling life is more possible when we bring our intentions into conscious view and work with them in a meaningful way. As you do the spiritual and emotional work offered here, you will hopefully find yourself more able to articulate these intentions, pay attention to them as they change, and put in the energy to realize them. If it is helpful, I encourage you to hone the intentions you have explored in the preceding chapters and write them down. Try to sculpt them into a simple statement that you can keep returning to.

In these next chapters, we will look at the business aspects of practicing, through a spiritual and emotional lens. Healing practitioners often push away these parts of sustaining their path because (1) they are so distinctly not what we think of when we talk about healing and (2) the skill set required to do them is quite different from the one you draw on to practice your actual healing work. Our work exists beyond the relatively short-lived life of any government, religion, or monetary system, extending to the beginning of human existence until the end of it; and although our ancestors were not building websites, they also weren't living in this time. So, let us move forward in our paths and adapt with integrity.

Engaging the Impasse

As you develop a practice and actually live the life of offering healing work, you will find yourself encountering obstacles that need to be worked through. When focusing on the material or business aspects of one's practice, it can be easy to miss the emotional and spiritual components of these obstacles. At times you may even find yourself in a situation that feels like an impasse—a murky, confusing, seemingly impossible situation that renders you unable to resolve it. Often when situations seem that opaque and impossible, it is a sign that a trauma or a significant developmental wound is triggered. If you ignore these situations, they can dramatically impact your ability to build or sustain a practice, as well as the level of satisfaction and meaning you find in your work. These impasses and obstacles are so vast and individualized, occurring in all areas of your practice, it would be wildly unfeasible to name them all here. What I want to offer you is *an approach to an impasse or obstacle, rather than a solution.*

How will you know that you are in an impasse? In trauma theory it is often said that trauma reduces creativity. Every time I hear this, it concerns me. In my opinion, trauma often inspires us to an immense level of creativity to endure life, both artistically and practically. To say that trauma makes us less creative is flat, lacking nuance, and a misunderstanding of the resiliency that individuals and communities employ to survive trauma. However, I think a more accurate read on this is that trauma can at times make us *feel* very trapped, as though certain aspects of life must be endured, rather than changed. Or it can inspire a sense that there is *only one* way something can be changed and if that is not possible then enduring suffering is the only other option. However, there is still immense creativity in *how* we endure suffering. Most of us live in a series of patterns, and over time you will hopefully build a knowing relationship to what yours are. For example, the person who overextends to help others when their own self-esteem is threatened can grow an awareness of this. Eventually they will no longer be bewildered by their exhaustion and compulsive acts of service, but rather aware that this is the strategy they use to bolster a wounded ego. Or the person who becomes irate and angry in response to failure eventually embraces the underlying shame the failure produces (that the anger defends against). Or the practitioner who exhausts themselves with manic overfunctioning each time they lose a client finds a way to pause and confront the fear underneath the doing-ness. From awareness comes the possibility to choose a new approach.

Our personal and collective traumas and developmental woundings inform how we deal with hardship. This could be anything from the collective trauma of experiencing racism to the personal developmental wound of being consistently criticized as a child. Contemporary trauma theory identifies five primary trauma responses to traumatic events.[6] Each of these responses can become habituated around emotions that one cannot self-regulate. These trauma responses are referenced by many names, but some common ones are: Freeze, Attach, Fight, Flight, and Submit. In addition to trauma theory, attachment theory offers a framework for further understanding your relationship to hardship. Attachment theory identifies certain attachment "styles" that explain how we maintain connections in our relationships, as well as how we regulate our emotions. Rather than explain trauma and attachment theory at length, what I want you to consider is that all of your behaviors under stress are *strategies for survival* and they were developed *in relationship to fear*. Human beings are vulnerable. Beneath all the daily chatter of our egos is the fear of death and the drive to live. As children we survive by staying safely connected to other humans, which results in a myriad of strategies to do so. We are complex emotional and psychological creatures and we must find ways to cope with overwhelming feelings. For example, if you were routinely overpowered with criticism as a child, to the point that you questioned if your caregivers loved you and wanted you, you may have been overwhelmed with fears of abandonment (because to a child abandonment = death). Your nervous system and complex psyche may have automatically (it is not a choice) dissociated in response to the criticism, making it difficult to take in feedback, yet tolerable to stay connected to someone who is harming you. Now as an adult healing practitioner, when you work with a critical client you find yourself somehow emotionally numb and struggling to access your skills. The unique ways that our psyches are organized inform how we deal with difficult and emotionally activating experiences. Whether working in a physical, psychological, or spiritual realm (or all three), healing practitioners work with people's pain, with real concerns about health and survival, all while trying to live amid capitalism. These are fear-inducing circumstances that are rooted in survival. Thus whatever survival strategies and fear-tolerating strategies you have, regardless of how wildly ineffective or not they are, will emerge in building your practice and offering your services.

Psychological development and spiritual development are intimately related, but they are not the same thing. Emotionally activating experiences can also be spiritually activating. Somewhere inside each of us, regardless of one's interest in spirituality, are spiritual questions that are inherent to humanity. Questions about morality, life, death, meaning, and purpose— these are spiritual questions. Engaging with questions like these requires presence and an ability to be with the unanswerable. It is hard to be present and curious with the unanswerable when one is busy coping with intolerable fear. However, practice is what creates new skills. In asking yourself what it means to live a meaningful life, to confront your own imminent death, to love despite knowing there will be loss—this is a practice of growing your ability to be present and tolerate fear.

Impasses typically occur when you employ your self-regulatory responses to stay safe in response to something that threatens, frightens, or overwhelms you. Sometimes we employ these responses because there is something happening in the moment that is dangerous. However, other times we respond in these ways because we are responding to a past trauma as though it is happening now, despite the current situation being nontraumatic. When trauma responses and attachment strategies are activated in situations that are not actually traumatic or wounding, they can inhibit growth and resolution to problems. If in response to building your practice or working with clients you feel frozen, anxious, numb, depressed, ashamed, in manic hyperdrive, highly irritable, or emotionally shut down *and you are not making any progress on this,* you might be activated and at an impasse.

Trauma theory is vast and there are many books that have already tackled the subject, but here are some brief descriptions of what trauma looks like when it either has become a habituated state of being or flares up in a full trauma state. If you relate to any of these, take some time to get curious about how they came to be, what sets them off, and the underlying needs or healing required to allow them to soften. When you reach an impasse, it will be incredibly useful to have self-knowledge about these. It is helpful and often necessary to have the support of someone who works with trauma to resolve these responses, so don't suffer in it alone, but rather reach out for some help.

Freeze Response

A freeze response is what activates during a traumatic event in which your nervous system has assessed in a fraction of a second that you are in incredible danger, but survival could be possible if you become very still, hypervigilantly alert, and maintain an immense amount of energy in your body, in case you need to fight or run.

Panic attacks, hypervigilance, constant orientation to things that could be dangerous, paranoia, skepticism, nervousness, and anxiety are all ways that a freeze response can become habituated. This can look like being highly anxious about something, vigilantly researching it or learning about it, but being quite unable to move into action about it. An example could be needing to set up a payment system for your practice and researching all the options, taking particular care to notice everything that could go wrong with each one, then making no movement to choose one as you continue with the ritual of researching them.

Attach Response

An attach response is what activates during a traumatic event in which your nervous system has assessed in a fraction of a second that you are in incredible danger, but survival could be possible if you cry out for help from someone else, like a caregiver who can protect you.

An attach response is about becoming safe through a relationship to a protector. It is characterized by need and being a very nonthreatening person. Attention-seeking, seeming incapable, needing rescue by others, and overseeking help are hallmarks of this response. This is a response that often engenders care from others. If you find yourself looking to others to solve problems, even when you might be capable enough to do it yourself, but it just feels soothing to have someone else do it for you—this might be part of your psychological structure. This response might sound lovely because people often want to help you, but in reality it relates to a lack of self-esteem, a lack of self-trust in your own capacity, and you are still living in endless fear that you won't be okay unless others help you. It can also be taxing on relationships to need this level of support from others.

Fight Response

A fight response is what activates during a traumatic event in which your nervous system has assessed in a fraction of a second that you are in incredible danger, but survival could be possible if you fight your way to safety.

Being highly judgmental of yourself or others, needing excessive amounts of control, getting into frequent arguments, feeling suicidal or homicidal, having overly strict boundaries, asserting protection for yourself or others, or self-harming/attacking the self are all ways that a habituated fight response may appear. Fight responses can be directed outward, but they can also be directed inward. For example, if you make a mistake in your practice that scares you—perhaps you lost some money and have trauma related to financial insecurity—and in response you berate yourself with negative self-talk, or physically self-harm with substances, overgrooming, skin-picking, self-hitting, or self-cutting.

Flight Response

A flight response is what activates during a traumatic event in which your nervous system has assessed in a fraction of a second that you are in incredible danger, but survival could be possible if you run or escape to safety.

Being avoidant, misusing substances, being independent, always needing a way out of situations, and struggling to commit to them are common ways that a flight response manifests. People with a habituated flight response sometimes struggle to build strong bonds in healing relationships because there can be so much inconsistency and lack of commitment. A flight response could look like becoming overwhelmed with the commitment and the people depending on you (perhaps you were traumatically engulfed by the needs of others in the past), and then closing down your practice or downsizing it (rather than finding ways to change how you run it).

Submit Response

A submit response is what activates during a traumatic event in which your nervous system has assessed in a fraction of a second that you are possibly going to die, but survival could be possible if you collapse and become completely nonthreatening or appear already dead. This response also protects you from pain, due to being largely dissociated from your physical body.

When this response is habituated it can look like depression, being easygoing, collapse, self-loathing, hopelessness, passivity, or self-sacrificing, and is characterized by shame. If in response to struggle within your practice you find yourself unable to do anything, this is quite possibly a habituated state for you. This could look like needing to make a phone call or do a simple task and taking weeks to accomplish it, feeling somehow unable to take action, despite being competent enough to complete the task when you aren't under stress.

* * *

As you read through these responses, you may feel sad, ashamed, or afraid the ways you relate to them mean something is wrong with you. But hold up—maintain some compassion for yourself. These are ways that you have learned to cope with unbearable situations, and these responses have pro-tected you. They are brilliant responses that exist within you to keep you alive. They make you human. Though they have become habituated and can cause difficulty, they are not a life sentence and they have positive, useful attributes as well (some of which I noted in the descriptions).

Increased understanding of your responses allows you some space to work with them and make it through impasses. While these trauma responses are a guide, as you learn more about trauma and attachment, remember not to flatten yourself. You are complex and have many emotions. You are not just "avoidant" or have only an "attach" response. You move in and out of these states depending on your previous life experience and the circumstances you exist in now.

In addition to trauma states, emotions have a complex life and relation-ship to each other even without trauma. When an injury isn't perceived by the body as life threatening, it is still perceived as wounding. From that space comes a series of other strategies for dealing with emotions.

While any emotion can be the prominent one in an impasse, expres-sions of anger are common—everything from mild complaining to rage. I am highlighting anger because it can feel less vulnerable than fear, sad-ness, or shame, and can thus be a protecting, cover emotion. People often say they feel angry when the core emotion is a more vulnerable one. Con-versely, people often say they are *not angry* when they actually are. Anger has a wide swath of nuances. Feeling frustrated, annoyed, irritated, or irked are all forms of anger. While anger can be destructive when unexplored or expressed through violence, it is an indispensable guide and teacher when listened to. Beloved anger tells us about our needs, our fears, our pain, and things we are ashamed of. In every complaint is a prayer, a hope, and a worry that needs may go unmet. However, while anger can teach us and guide us, it is also a very powerful emotion and it needs to be metabolized effectively or it can be destructive. What does it mean to metabolize an emotion? Emotions have lives of their own, and they truly have needs. Emotions need to be (1) felt, (2) understood or witnessed, and (3) expressed. When they do not receive these three things, they are not metabolized or digested and can stay in a more raw and unconscious form. Much as when food goes undigested, you do not receive its nutrients to fuel you. Unmetabolized emotions are rendered meaningless, which is not to say they go without purpose, but rather that the powerful meaning of them is not known or harnessed. Because shame, fear, powerlessness, and grief can be so intimately connected to anger, it can be useful to be curious about what other emotions you may be protecting or obscuring with anger.

In regard to metabolizing emotions, some people struggle with the difference between feeling an emotion and expressing it. Feeling an emotion is something that happens internally. It is an awareness of the sensations, the thoughts, the behaviors, and the energy of an emotion. Expressing an emotion is an outward release. It can be actions such as crying, laughing, shaking, or voicing words in an embodied way. Most of us know the feeling of anxiety. And most of us are familiar with the feeling of anxiety that won't release but sticks around for a long time, also known as stress. As you may have experienced with anxiety: only feeling an emotion will not metabolize it. Expressing anxiety in, for example, the form of crying or shaking can lead to metabolizing it. On some level your body knows what to do to metabolize feelings. Often it is as simple as getting out of your own way and letting the expression happen. Because of individual and cultural wounding and conditioning, many of us stop ourselves from expressing emotions. This is very common in the case of crying. Crying is such a great release and yet many people refuse to let themselves cry, which results in the very uncomfortable experience of an emotion that persists without relief. Being witnessed or understood is what shifts an emotional expression into an understandable and observable event. This can be a small, internal event of self-witnessing or a larger event of being witnessed by another person or even by a group. When I say "witnessed" or "understood," I use those terms in a very specific way. The kind of witnessing that metabolizes an emotion is compassionate, nonjudgmental, and does not deflect blame onto other people. Being witnessed by someone who is judging you or, conversely, taking your "side" (judging someone else) in order to be "supportive" does not metabolize emotions. For big emotions of a confusing nature that include substantial wounding or trauma, we often need some form of witnessing or understanding from a wise, caring other. Great healing can come from just being understood and held in positive regard.

The first step in confronting an impasse is *curiosity*. True curiosity requires expansive thinking, without judgment. You only need to start where you are. In this next example, rather than explain a lesson from the place of having already learned it, I am going to walk you through an experience from the muddled perspective I had while encountering and understanding it. Hopefully you can see how it started to metabolize.

At some point after my first few years of practicing therapy, I noticed a growing irritation with certain clients. Some of the people I worked with would show up to their sessions without fail, and give me ample notice when they would not be in attendance. However, some would cancel every few weeks with no reason, or not show up at all and expect an exception around paying a cancellation fee, or cancel with reasons such as: "I want to go to dinner with a friend that night instead." I found myself feeling irritated and judgmental of these people—they didn't care about therapy, they were inconsiderate, they were entitled! I felt trapped and unable to do anything to change the situation. I felt I couldn't possibly tell them this was not okay, because that would be too controlling. Who was I to say what is a valid reason to cancel versus invalid? I told myself I was just beholden to these inconsiderate people; and all I could do was hope that perhaps if I worked harder with them, they would see the value and start prioritizing showing up. I spent months feeling annoyed and complaining to my colleagues, who had very similar complaints about their own practices. We would perform our regular commiseration rituals and collude in the idea that this was just a normal part of our paths.

There were a few people in my practice who really tested me. And in a sense, they offered me an opportunity to really know my own needs. I became curious—*Why do these people irritate me so much? What about this situation doesn't work?* I started to become aware that I was not only annoyed, but I was anxious. Each week I would anxiously await the possible phone call announcing a cancellation. Then I would anxiously call back to remind them they still had to pay for the appointment because the cancellation was only an hour before the session. Or I would become filled with anxiety when I came to the waiting room to find no one was there—*Were they late? How long should I wait? Are they not coming at all?* It dawned on me *this was not good for them either.* I was not present and engaged with their needs; I was anxious and focused on mine. I was scared about my unstable income, upset about my wasted time, and resentful when I would turn away new clients because I did not have space for them, yet I maintained space for people who didn't even use it. I needed to find a way through this, or it would be a detriment to their therapy and my well-being. It was a personal issue, an issue that impacted them, and a logistical issue, because I cannot sustain a practice when people don't show up to work with me.

I started to bring these concerns to my personal therapy and dive deep into my own wounding to understand my response. There were many aspects to this situation that didn't work for me and that brought up old pain, but here are the really big ones that illustrate moving through an impasse: I felt ashamed to have needs, I felt afraid of being attacked if I made any boundaries or requests, and I could not offer meaningful therapy while I was so preoccupied with my own shame and fear.

What are the next steps beyond curiosity when in an impasse space? *Asking for help, being willing to change, and accruing new skills or knowledge.*

ASKING FOR HELP: Certainly I was not the first person to have my boundaries about time and money tested in the healing relationship. Through connecting to colleagues and mentors, and doing my own growth work, I was able to do more than complain and blame my clients, but rather to make an "I" statement and say: "I don't know what to do. I feel ashamed, angry, and afraid that what I need is too much to ask for. I need help making it through this." The problem wasn't that my clients pushed on the boundaries or that I didn't work hard enough for them to value the time. It was that I was not telling them what I expect and need in order to function as their therapist.

People come to us for healing because they need help, and sometimes they tell you about what they need in confusing and unconscious ways. You cannot expect your clients to already know how to be in relationship to you without you expressing your needs to them. This is the foundation of getting to know another person and develop intimacy. Many of these clients were silently screaming at me for help, and I wasn't able to hear them. They were saying: "I have no idea how to do therapy. Does it work if I cancel regularly?" "I am afraid I don't mean anything to you, and the only way I know how much I impact you is when I experiment with not showing up." "It feels unbearable to be seen by you, so I cancel to manage my fears of exposure." And on and on. There are so many underlying reasons clients push on our needs, in many different types of healing practices. The more I stopped trying to push away my own needs and asked for help, the more I could hear the pain in clients' actions and further help them. My colleagues and mentors gave me guidance on how to value my own needs and communicate with compassion about the guidelines of the therapy relationship. I was able to metabolize the anger, fear, and shame by more deeply owning that I have needs and there isn't anything wrong with that. When I decided to start communicating about this issue with my clients, I remember one colleague suggested to me that I don't make it about my own needs, that I make it about their need for therapy. But that isn't the whole truth and it isn't a full metabolizing of the emotions. It is partially a projection of my own needs onto them. For therapy to be effective they needed to show up, but I also needed a sense that the relationship was stable enough that I could trust them to prioritize the work and compensate me; otherwise, I would be too anxious to be their therapist. It is easy to get into the habit of pretending that as a healing practitioner you are so giving that you do not need anything in return, but what other job cancels your workday after you already showed up and then refuses to pay you? There is no need to run your own practice with such little regard for yourself.

BEING WILLING TO CHANGE: It is so comfortable and unbearable to stay the same. When we don't take the risk to change, we know what kind of suffering to expect: it is the same thing we've been tolerating our whole life. And yet lack of movement and growth is agitating. The risk you run by not changing is a life full of dissatisfaction, regrets, and further ingraining preexisting wounds. While change typically involves loss, it often indicates growth toward something that is a better fit. When I finally did make more boundaries in my practice, I lost some clients. Some people were not ready to change with me. However, because of my courage to speak about the dynamic, the people who were willing to explore their reasons for canceling and their fears around connection were greatly assisted in their growth. And I no longer felt agitated, ashamed, or afraid going into my sessions, which allowed me to offer far superior work.

ACCRUING NEW SKILLS OR KNOWLEDGE: After you have been curious, asked for help, and established a will to change, you will need the skills and knowledge to implement the change. In the case of my story, speaking truth to an uncomfortable dynamic was a skill that I had to develop. Knowing myself enough to be clear on what I need to function as a healer is self-knowledge. Understanding the relationship between needs, shame, and aggression is knowledge. Being able to tolerate the responses that others had to my needs, even if they were negative, was a skill. This process forced me to grow immensely. After having these kinds of conversations several times, it becomes second nature and much easier for you to call on in future situations. I no longer feel overwhelming fear about someone repeatedly canceling on me, because I feel comfortable saying I can't effectively work under those circumstances.

It is important to hold that it is okay to change. There may be ways you set up your healing practice in the beginning that will not work for you eternally. Perhaps some of your clients worked with you when you were fresh out of training and more insecure, fumbling to value your own offerings. You do not have to be the same person forever, and you model self-compassion and self-generosity by allowing your clients to see you grow. It is humbling to work with the same person for many years, just as it is humbling to have any long-term relationship.

The above example explores an impasse related to several clients and a larger approach to how I was holding my work. However, impasses emerge in the mundane logistics of running a practice as well. Anytime you procrastinate beyond reason or have tasks you continually avoid, there is an opportunity to be curious—is this an impasse? What is standing in the way of movement? Everything in life can be imbued with larger spiritual and emotional meaning. Your practice will benefit from meaningfully engaging with these spiritual and emotional aspects, even when it comes to small logistics. You can employ the same approach as discussed above: (1) curiosity, (2) asking for help, (3) being willing to change, and (4) accruing new skills or knowledge. An example of logistics being imbued with deeper meaning can be seen in relationship to websites. In supporting people to build their practices, I have seen a common struggle emerge around the daunting task of creating an online presence. I have watched practitioners do everything from denying they need a website to building an entire website and refusing to publish it. Telling yourself that you are ridiculous for postponing the publishing of your website is ignoring the deeper emotional and spiritual meaning of the task. Even though publishing a completed website is one click of a button, it is also a modern-day rite of passage that symbolizes a step in self-actualization and a big risk related to the exposure inherent in being seen. It takes a lot of confidence to announce one's role to the world and assert one's skills. Websites serve as a declaration of offerings, and anyone can look at them, including all of your family members, your exes, and people you went to middle school with who remember your full name.

An additional note on logistics: it is useful to acknowledge that everything in life can be broken down into smaller tasks. Embarking on your path, learning the skills of your craft, developing a thriving practice, and then maintaining that practice all takes time and it is overwhelming if you think about this as one task. In the example of creating a website, don't let that be one item on your to-do list, because it is actually several. In the creation of a website you must research platforms, choose and take photos, write the copy, organize information, have peers review it, and on and on. Wherever you become stuck in a task, ask yourself what the very next, small step is in completing it and focus on that. The next small step might be that you need to eat lunch before you continue your work. By breaking logistics down into smaller steps, you are navigating smaller challenges.

EXERCISES AND EXPERIENTIALS
CHAPTER 6

6.1 *Writing*

1. Can you think of any experiences in your life that were impasses? What did you do to find your way through them? How do you feel about the way you made it through? Try writing a longer narrative about this or have a friend interview you in depth about the experience, as a way to connect with the nuances of it.

2. In writing a personal narrative of a previous impasse, describe how you engaged with each of these steps: being curious, asking for help, being willing to change, and accruing new skills or knowledge.

3. How are you at metabolizing your emotions? Do you feel them? Do you express them? Do you give compassionate witnessing and understanding to yourself or receive it from others?

4. How are you at being curious about a situation while having big feelings?

5. How are you at asking for help?

6. What is it like for you to make changes in relationships or logistics? Are you flexible, adaptable, or more rigid?

7. How is it for you to admit or realize that you need to grow or accrue new skills or knowledge to make it through a difficult situation?

6.2 *Sharing and Witnessing*

With a trusted friend, colleague, or community member, share about something you are reflecting on in regards to a personal impasse. This could be something you need help with, something you want to grow around, or something you desire. Try being vulnerable. When you are sharing, challenge yourself to stay present in your body as you speak. Notice what it is like to be witnessed and to be vulnerable.

Communicating the Essential

(or The Deconstruction of Marketing and Branding)

Thus far we have covered several aspects related to identifying and stepping into the path of your healing practice. After attaining a certain level of clarity about your path, it is time to work on the fundamentals of how you will actually connect with the people you will support in healing. Of course, there are deep emotional and spiritual issues that emerge in that attempt at connection.

Marketing and branding are widely used terms to describe strategies for selling a product, or selling an idea that leads to the sale of a product. The process of finding people who will compensate you for your services does not need to be spiritually harmful or corrupt, though these concepts carry a spiritually harmful and corrupt historical and contemporary narrative. You could view your practice through this lens: you are selling an idea—it could be something like wellness or healing—and that leads to the sale of your product, your services. However, the concepts of marketing and branding often center capitalism: the notion that the highest intention is to sell at an ever-increasing rate, with the ultimate intention being mass accumulation of wealth, with little to no regard for the impact on the producer (you and others, if you have employees) or the consumer (the people you offer services to).

Humans are very responsive to fear and shame, and thus marketing and branding often attempt to elicit these emotions or promise relief from them. For example, narratives such as *aging is ugly* or *owning an older car is embarrassing* can be followed up with a solution: *buy an anti-aging product* or *buy a new car.* Along with the shame and fear, people are also instructed to consume at a rate that is destroying our planet and collective health: *you already own a car that works fine, but there is nothing wrong with ignoring the impact that producing new cars has on the environment, and you should buy a new one.* Under the dominant paradigms of marketing guidance, you may find yourself being encouraged to engage in several types of marketing, with an aggressive tone, and playing on people's fears. Unsurprisingly, those types of marketing are very effective. If you want to make more money than you ever need in this lifetime, that is definitely the strategy you should use. However, it is not in integrity with your path. Terrifying someone into buying a service, because they won't ever find happiness without it, is spiritually bereft. The method in this book is not about becoming wildly rich or selling people things they do not need. Approaching marketing with a different lens leaves you open to connect with the people you work with from a place of integrity.

In deconstructing and reframing these concepts, we can start with the intention behind them. While typical marketing and branding advice may be about trying to sell as much product as possible, that doesn't have to be *your* intention. Your actual intentions may vary, and I encourage you to explore what they are. Note that it could be as simple as: finding the people you will offer healing work to and being sustained by that exchange without causing unnecessary harm. Being "sustained" can refer to many needs (e.g., meaning, a sense of purpose, safety, emotional sustenance), but within a capitalist system it most certainly means making money. When you seek out advice related to marketing and branding, you can always weigh it against your intentions in an effort to discern if the advice is relevant to you and in integrity with your practice.

The next step in recontextualizing these concepts is to strip them down to the bare essentials. Marketing in its most basic form is just communication. It is communication that is highly strategic, but at the end of the day it is telling someone about a product or service. Branding in its most basic form is taking the essence of your belief system or your medicine and orienting all your communications toward expressing it. Branding in the mainstream capitalist sense is about creating an image or an idea and selling that. It generally pertains to the design of the advertising and the product, and the overall flavor of how a product is displayed to the world. Most cars are pretty similar, but car branding is not. Behind car advertising is everything from selling a sense of personal freedom and strength to selling a sense of security that your family will easily survive any car accident without injury. Branding works because we are spiritual beings and we are moved by our shared values and emotional truths. In a nutshell, when someone creates branding and marketing that says, "We value health and wellness," other people who share that value resonate with the marketing. Of course, there is quite a bit of nuance within value systems; and while "We value health and wellness" is a broad statement, actual marketing tends to get very specific and tailored to a particular subset of people.

And finally, as healing practitioners orienting to these concepts, we need to talk about integrity. There are many values that get communicated less directly in branding, through what is not explicitly said. An advertisement might not say it, but when a health and wellness ad campaign only uses images of, for example, able-bodied, wealthy, thin people, the campaign could be interpreted as saying: we value the health and wellness of able-bodied, wealthy, thin people. Or in another example, advertisements for airline flights might express a value of freedom and exploration to "exotic" or "undiscovered" places (where Indigenous people have lived for thousands of years); however, what is not said might be something like: we value ignoring the horrific legacy of colonialism and the devastating environmental impact of airline travel that is destroying the "pure" or "pristine" nature that the customer will visit on their trip. Some marketing and branding is harming in a purposeful way, whereas some does it from an unconscious or fantasy-based place. (Imagining that the natural world requires no stewardship by humans and is not negatively impacted by us is a fantasy that relieves us of the pain and guilt inherent in this ever-growing profound loss.) When we communicate about our values, we do so about our conscious *and* unconscious ones. What I want to invite you to do is create a form of communication and an expression of the essence of your belief system that is nonshaming, non-fear-inducing, an offering rather than an extraction, and to the best of your ability generally nonharming. Healing work is never grounded in the need to harm people. In its essence it is about undoing, transforming, and preventing harm. There is no need to communicate the essence of what you want to offer the world in a harming way.

Spiritual Communication

You are here on this earth to do something powerful, and you need to find the people you are going to do that with. My point in these last few paragraphs is to invite you to toss away the concepts of marketing and branding and replace those with what it is that you actually have to do: communicate the essential values and offerings you bring to the table. Remember your "why" that we covered earlier in this book? Now is the time to bring that in. Remember your niche or your prayer? Now is the time to bring that in. Communicating about yourself to the world is not just a matter of getting the basic logistics onto a business card or a website. It is about reaching deep inside of yourself and presenting the core of why you do this work, the hope that you hold for humanity, and the intentions that guide you. You are asking people to take a vulnerable step toward you, and you are meeting their vulnerability with yours. You do not need to share beyond comfort, and you should always respect your personal boundaries, but people do need to understand the guiding principles of your healing practice. From that place they can actually *choose you,* because there is *something to choose.* Remaining vague, unarticulated, or lackluster leaves people with nothing to grasp and nothing to say "yes" to.

Communication Issues

Communicating about your offerings, prayer, or niche is essential to meaningful engagement with your path. Many of us have "communication issues," and this can impact your ability to build a practice. Communication involves being able to articulate yourself or your offerings to others in a way that they can understand and receive. It requires confidence and clarity. If you struggle to feel confident, struggle to know yourself, feel uncomfortable being seen or asking for your needs to be met, worry about how others perceive you, or fear criticism and rejection, you might struggle to communicate with the world. Some common themes underlying communication issues are lack of relationship with self (resulting in not knowing your needs), low self-esteem (resulting in not valuing your needs or contributions), and relational anxiety (resulting in feeling afraid of how others will respond to you).

If you struggle to know your needs in the first place or struggle to know what you are offering to others, working with these themes can be a great foundational place to explore building a more involved relationship with your inner world. These are steps that have to occur before you can communicate to the people you want to work with. You can do this work the same way you would get to know anyone: conversation with yourself, being curious about yourself, paying attention to yourself. This might sound difficult if you have never done it, and it is—it often requires a lot of work to get to know someone. Journaling, meditating, or actually talking to yourself are great ways to get more curious and develop a richer inner-knowing. Psychotherapy is also an excellent avenue for knowing yourself in a deeper way.

If you struggle with low self-esteem, you might be a healing practitioner who has made it to the point that you have "enough" clients, but your practice may not reflect what you need in other ways. Your client base might not be the people you feel called to work with, you might not be compensated reasonably, you might not communicate to the world what you actually need to be sustained, or you might be downplaying what you have to offer and staying small. It may sound strange, but your communication to those you want to work with needs to be imbued with *your* needs and gifts. When you communicate what you offer, you are also communicating what you need and what sustains you—that communication is not just for the person receiving it; it is for you as well. Healers who suffer from self-esteem issues often overidentify with giving, feeling that it is wrong to express our needs in the healing relationship or that we do not deserve to have needs, which in turn just depletes us and diminishes what we can actually offer.

Relational anxiety occurs when you feel afraid to be yourself and to speak about your needs around others. It often stems from being punished, criticized, engulfed, ignored, or dismissed for having needs or for who you are (which is in essence a need to be accepted). Understanding and accepting your needs is a critical part of feeling comfortable with communicating your offerings. If someone criticizes you or punishes you for having needs, you can simply not work with them; or in the case of people whose healing work involves supporting emotional growth, it can become a fruitful opportunity to explore why this person feels compelled to attack someone for having needs or limits. Similar to issues with self-esteem, this is where many healing practitioners get stuck—it feels vulnerable to offer services and ask to be compensated for them. You are not only offering a service; you are also asking to be cared for in exchange. In a global economy fueled by shame, it can be hard to love yourself enough to claim your true place in the world, free from fear of how others will respond. I want to support you in the fullest liberation of your being and your path. A prayer said without conviction is just words.

As humans, we all have needs and must get them met, and we all have an essence or a personality that wants to be expressed. So, if you don't feel at ease communicating your needs, you have likely found some other ways to deal with the necessity of communication in relationship to others. It could be that you are self-reliant and try to manage all your needs and meet them without telling others. It could be that you engage in self-neglect and try to survive with most of your needs going unmet. It could be that you project your needs onto others, and then try to fulfill "their needs," which in turn meet your own (because they were yours in the first place). Whatever your relationship to your own needs is, it is critical to understand this as you embark on a path where your survival is dependent on your being able to know and communicate them.

Fearing rejection or judgment holds many people back from communicating in the way I am describing. And you know what? Some people will judge you. Some people will reject you. Some people are going to hate this book, but I still wrote it. Because some people will feel met, understood, supported, and able to take the next steps in their life. Your medicine is a balm, and you are communicating to the people who need it, not the people who don't.

Working with Yourself, Not against Yourself

We all communicate in different ways and have different levels of comfort in how we share the most intimate parts of our belief systems and our craft. Some of us want to shout it out on the rooftops, some of us want to carefully share in more intimate settings, and then others want to write in the privacy of their own homes with little in-person interaction. None of these methods is better or worse; they are just different. These forms of communication could be the way you invite people to work with you, or they could be how you actually work with people. You might write a blog to connect with potential clients, or you might just write a blog and that is the medicine you offer. While growing and changing are essential parts of maintaining your path, it is also crucial to honor who you are and the real limits or edges you work within. If giving public lectures causes you to have a panic attack followed by a three-day shame spiral, remember that you don't have to do public speaking. Or you might want to think creatively about what kind of public speaking works; for example: being in a contained smaller class size that develops a bond over several weeks, rather than a large event with people you have no ongoing connection to. If speaking off the cuff produces immense anxiety and you prefer the written word, which can be carefully curated over time, you might forgo in-person avenues completely. There are many ways to communicate your essential offerings to people. My recommendations are:

1. Find a few ways to communicate that are compatible with your personality; even just one single form of communication done well can be enough.

2. Hone those forms of communication and heighten your skill level with them.

There are five main methods of communicating to people you want to work with:

1. Online presence

2. Networking

3. Word of mouth

4. Free offerings

5. Advertising

We are going to get deep into each of these in the next chapter, but first I want to stress that you do not have to do all of these things. Remember that whatever form of communication you choose, this is your life. You will be doing this often. Don't choose something you despise doing. If you truly thrive being in regular contact with community, become depressed when you spend too much time on a computer, and enjoy the intensity of articulating yourself on the spot, don't choose communication methods that isolate you. Some "marketing" guidance will tell you that certain tactics are a must and that you will not survive without them. Others will assert that you have to be strong on several tactics, having an aggressive multipronged approach. That simply is not true. Remember, you aren't trying to serve one billion hamburgers or run a global franchise with a multibillion-dollar annual revenue stream. Your "product" is your own energy. You don't need to convince people to buy something from you that they don't actually need. Your job is just to communicate with people who want and need your services in a style that doesn't burn you out.

After you hone in on what you like doing and commit to it, it is important to do it well. If all you are going to use to communicate with the world is word of mouth, you need to be a very well-networked person. Or perhaps you are strongly introverted and only want to have a website—make sure that website is incredible and that you have done the work to make it effective. Having a subpar website, a somewhat-connected word-of-mouth network, plus a social media account you reluctantly intermittently use is a lot of energy going out without a finely crafted and cohesive result. It takes a lot of effort and time to do something well.

Starting a Conversation Doesn't Mean You Cannot Exit It

Communication with the world requires protection. You may be a powerful healer, but you are not immune to having your own limits. By communicating your offerings you are starting conversations with many people. All of those people will be coming to you with unconscious material. Some of that unconscious material will not be appropriate for you to engage with. Healing practitioners work in a messy business. We deal with issues that drive people to their most vulnerable parts and that at times can produce disturbing behavior. People also come to us in intense need. That level of need, possibly even desperation, can make people act aggressively or harmfully. Each of us has these parts of ourselves, and to say that people come to us with their messy parts does not imply that we do not also have our messy parts. In fact, your messiness is part of why you need protection. All of us have limits, and people we cannot work with. These concerning dynamics can even start to appear in the initial communication phase, before you have started working with someone. When we do not honor those limits is when our own disturbing and messy behaviors emerge.

A clear and classic example of this is: have you ever heard the adage "Don't read the comments"? If you are a blogger, a vlogger, use social media, or post any content on the internet, then you have probably seen that there is almost always a section for the consumers of the content to leave a comment. Many healing practitioners use online platforms to share about their work. If you are lucky, most of the time you will get comments that are grateful or at worst tell you about a technical error or give meaningful feedback. In my experience the comments that are more uncomfortable to read run anywhere from straight-up harassment to long-winded, invasive explanations of someone's personal material that they then want advice on from the original poster via the comments section. This can be upsetting for the practitioner and, in more extreme situations, bring out our messier parts. Thus the saying: "Don't read the comments."

There can be a whole host of issues that come with opening up conversations with people not yet known to you, and it is important to remember that just because you are in a conversation doesn't mean that you cannot end it or have needs around it. If you are a person who really struggles to make boundaries with others or protect yourself, you may find that, as a means of protection, you are averse to putting yourself out there. Part of communicating your offerings is about knowing your own limits and needs.

Some people may find that they truly need a higher level of protection. I have listened to endless hours of healing practitioners complaining about being asked medical, emotional, and spiritual questions in every venue of public life. I once even had a roommate who announced a few days into living together that she was excited to live with us (two healing practitioners) so she could receive healing support. Needless to say, we felt used and irritated at the assumption. In retrospect, my healer-roommate and I were very early in our careers, and I don't think we had a solid appreciation for how much protection we needed as healers. Our work is grounded in integrity and a commitment to serve, but that doesn't mean you have to offer your gifts to whatever random person texts you a photo of their foot fungus at 1 a.m. for herbal suggestions and at-home remedies. For many reasons some of us are magnets for vampiric exchanges, or struggle so much to make boundaries, that the boundary needs to be built into the communication method itself. For example: setting a boundary when someone sends you an email that is invasive or hurtful is different from when someone does that in person. While offering a free in-person class is a great way for people to connect with you, it also requires some comfort dealing with whoever shows up.

A few years ago I offered a training, and afterward one of the participants expressed wanting to work with me as their therapist. I told them my practice was full, but that I would be happy to give them a referral. They felt certain they had to work with me and asked me to call them when I had space. When I let them know that I don't keep a waiting list, they became upset, started to criticize how I run my practice, and finally asked in an angry tone, "Well, how is anyone supposed to work with you then?!" The answer to that question is: "anyone" cannot work with me. I am a human being and I choose who I work with. If my practice is full, I cannot suddenly conjure up more capacity just because someone wants me to.

In order to work in a public sphere, where I encounter complete strangers, I have had to build a lot more capacity and strategy regarding saying "no" or ending conversations. There is a limit to how much I can do that without feeling drained; for that reason, I also cherish types of communication that have boundaries built in and allow more time to respond. However, if I felt these harder interactions were so derailing for me that it was unsustainable, I would likely not teach in person at all, letting my "communication of my services" or my actual services be something where I always had more control and space to respond.

Beyond just being annoying, some of these exchanges can impact you in significantly harmful ways. In order for you to feel safe enough to keep putting yourself out there, continue to enjoy the process of communicating with potential clients, and prevent vicarious trauma, you will need to be able to say "no." As a trauma specialist, a regular part of my life is people trying to tell me about atrocious violence and wanting nonconsensual emotional support in uncontained spaces—over email, at a party, at the grocery store, while I am getting a haircut. It takes vital energy to be in conversation with people who come to you for your services (or who come to you because of who you are, even if they don't want to use your services). Being able to honor your limits (I cannot listen to the worst traumas that have happened to every person who feels like sharing that with me) allows you to be sustained in the work.

These are some of the emotional underpinnings of communicating your offerings to the world. It takes time to build an adequate layer of protection around you and feel confident in maintaining it. It takes self-exploration and self-acceptance to honor the ways that you communicate best. From your general life experiences, you probably already know a lot about what makes it hard for you to say "no," which types of communications drain you and which types enliven you, and how you respond to invasive or difficult interactions. Your existing self-knowledge is a good place to start, because it will likely show up in some similar ways in your healing practice.

EXERCISES AND EXPERIENTIALS

CHAPTER 7

7.1 *Conversation*

Set up a time to talk with a fellow healing practitioner or a friend and consider discussing the following:

1. How do you feel about communicating your practice to the world?

2. What was your preexisting notion of marketing and branding?

3. How can your preexisting understanding expand or be further in integrity with your path?

4. What anxieties do you have about communicating your essential offerings?

5. What is it like for you to say "no" to someone who wants your help?

7.2 *Writing*

1. What do you know about yourself as a communicator?

2. What issues come up for you around having needs?

3. How do you feel about expressing yourself and having that expression seen by others?

4. Who taught you how, or where did you learn about having needs?

5. Who taught you how, or where did you learn about self-expression?

6. Reflecting on this chapter and your answers, where do you need growth and what is the next step in your process?

7.3 *Body Scan*

Using the same body scan from chapter 1 (or do a shorter version by focusing on your breath, your heart/chest, and your belly), ask yourself the question: how do I truly feel about publicly being a healing practitioner? Notice the sensations that emerge when you keep this question in mind. Be curious about the feelings and thoughts attached to those sensations. If any memories pop up, take note.

Methods of Communication

I have been asked numerous times why I use the term "prayer" when I talk about spirituality. People have questioned me, in a shocked tone, "Do you *really* pray?" Many of my ancestors were Christians, and before that they were polytheists practicing earth-based spiritualities primarily in what is now Western Europe. As someone with a European lineage, who has existed in politically radical spaces for all of my adult life, I can *completely* empathize with the surprise that I would use a term with so much baggage attached to it. By baggage, I mean: abuse of power. While I am an outspoken critic against Christian supremacy and recognize the ways it benefits from and fuels a symbiotic relationship with white supremacy, colonialism, and capitalism, I do not believe Christianity owns prayer (and I acknowledge that there are some very compassionate and loving Christians invested in the liberation of all people). As with many beliefs, rituals, or practices that are associated with Christianity, the act of what we call "prayer" in the English language pre-dates Christianity, existing in many cultures that Christianity has participated in colonizing. You can call it prayer, talking to spirit, setting intentions, casting spells, or by whatever name suits you—no religion owns the sacred act of communicating with spirit.

When you communicate your purpose and hope for and to the world, you are communicating your sacred offerings. There are multiple ways that you can do this and, with all things sacred, it is an ongoing practice rather than a single event. There are five main methods of communicating to people you want to offer your services to:

1. An online presence, typically in the form of a website or social media

2. Networking

3. Word of mouth

4. Free offerings, typically in the form of classes, written materials, and social media content

5. Advertising

In this chapter, we will take a look at each of these and explore what they mean in the context of maintaining a healing practice. Every aspect of your practice can be a spiritual process, and despite whatever each of these methods connotes to you, they are the methods of communication in this realm, and you can bring magic and a sacred intention to each of them.

Websites and Social Media, or Your Prayer in the Digital Age

Here is the short version of my thoughts on websites: it's not 1980, and you need a website. If you have older mentors, they may wax poetic on how they built a healing practice with no website. However, they have a referral network twenty-five years or more in the making. Their guidance doesn't reflect the space you currently inhabit. However, some people still build practices without a website, so if you truly do not want one, it is possible to go forth without. If that describes you, my only suggestion is to consider why you do not want one and be sure that choice is grounded in an embodied decision, rather than a reaction to fear.

While I don't adore the digital age, it's the one we live in. You can approach your website or social media presence from a spiritual lens: it is a "prayer" in the digital age, where you speak your truth and offer it for others to know.

Websites are complicated and require a lot of background knowledge to make useful. At minimum, it can be a business card: it has to be given to someone for them to know about it. This happens through you or others forwarding a link to your website to the person you want to look at it. However, the other way that people find information online is through *searching*. There is actually a lot of theory and technique involved in making your online presence *searchable*. That means you cannot simply make a website or start a social media account and expect people will instantly be directed to it when they start searching topics related to your offerings. With regard to websites, this is called Search Engine Optimization (SEO). People use search engines to find relevant web pages on the internet, and you have to take several actions to optimize your website to be found. SEO techniques change often, so there is no point detailing how it works here, but just know—it is very useful to learn about this, or if someone else is building your website, to make certain they know about this. With regard to social media, the process of being found is also far more complex than just making an account and starting to post. Each platform will require different techniques to make yourself visible; and if you go this route, just know that taking the time to understand how these systems work will make the effort you put in more impactful.

Beyond the behind-the-scenes optimization of your online presence is the most important part: the actual content. This tends to be where people get very stuck, for days and sometimes years. If you have any level of social or relational anxiety, self-doubt, fear of being seen, fear of having needs, fear of being mediocrè, issues with shame, or any other reason that you hold yourself back, then creating the content of your online presence will be an emotional journey. But remember, it is a *journey* not a single moment. Being in a frozen fear state about claiming your space in the world today doesn't mean you will be in that state in a week. You are an ever-growing being, and some things may need to heal to produce the content and put it out there.

In the content you create, you need to express your intentions and offerings, but there are a few things that are universally important as healers.

People come to us when we appear safe and strong enough to face their pain. However you do that needs to be communicated. Strength looks different for everyone. You might show your strength with softness or grace, or you might show it with an unfiltered expression of truth. There is no right way, but it is foundational to a healing practice. You don't necessarily need to state these things outright; communication happens in the subtleties of words, images, or the general tone of your content.

When I think about strength and safety, I go back to clarity and confidence. Clarity, being able to see with clearness rather than operate from an unconscious or unknowing place, creates safety. Confidence is the act of knowing your true skills and offering them without apology for who you are. Your prayers are not a place where you apologize for existing, apologize for taking up space, apologize for offering, or apologize for having the audacity to think you have value. They are also not a place where you need to fill the crevices of every sentence with words meant to prove you are worthy—which simultaneously illustrate you don't believe it. If you spend your time trying to hide due to fear, people will not be able to find you. Every layer of self-doubt or self-hatred must be stripped away. The content of your prayers just needs to be your true essence and your medicine—and that is not just "good enough"; *it is a wonderful gift.*

Of course, we all have ups and downs in our lives and it is impossible to maintain that pure state of self-love at all times. When you create your content, when you do your healing work, you enter a sacred space. How do you do this? Intention. Whatever you do to access the highest part of yourself, the ways that you get into sacred space, do that to create this content. If you sing, dance, practice ritual, rest, cook a family recipe, or do any other activity, work from that space. Trying to cram writing your entire website into lunch breaks at your second job while you are stressed out and hungry isn't going to cut it. This is a rite of passage; give yourself the gift of time and grounded presence.

Half of the art of communication is saying something other people can hear, and knowing who you are speaking to. If you have great things to say but they are presented in a disorganized manner that is difficult to access or read, a barrier is created for people who have vision issues, attention issues, or are at a level of distress that limits their ability to navigate technology. Consider the state people are in when they make their way to your web presence. Are they hurting? Are they seeking relief? Are they hopeful? You will want to write your content to them and no one else. This is a place where your "shadow-whys" can sometimes take over. A number one issue that comes up in public presence is wanting to curate one's identity in a certain way. As I spoke about in chapter 3, many practitioners use language that is either field-specific jargon or so technical that it requires someone to have training in their specific modality to understand. This often comes from a place of wanting to sound smart. However, remember that the language you use needs to be something that helps people feel *you*, not your degree. Colleagues may read your website, but they are not going to assume you aren't intelligent because you used accessible language. Another common issue is wanting to say things that friends, family, or other close people will approve of. Yet, those are not the people you are speaking to. The content you create here is a direct communication with the people you are called to serve. Other people can read it, but you are not writing it for them.

Content isn't just the words; it's the tone, the images, and every aspect of what you put out there. You get to creatively imbue each piece of your content with the underlying values that guide you, and make them cohesively fit together in a harmonious expression of your offerings.

If you practice a type of healing that is commonly understood, you do not need to create excess stress through trying to explain it or having several sections of your website focused on the theory behind it. If you practice a lesser-known healing modality, it may be helpful to potential clients for you to explain what you offer with more depth. Though still keep in mind that the majority of people are not coming to you because of the description you gave of evidence for how your healing system was developed, or because your modality has been approved by a professional association. They are coming to you because they got a feel for you, you really came through, and they felt a connection with the human you are, with your beliefs and values.

Make it easy for people to contact you. This is so, so important. I cannot tell you how many healers create an online presence that requires a small detective mission to find their contact info. Whatever your main contact is— email, phone, direct messages through a social media app—make that very clear so people don't have to struggle to connect with you.

This is a rite of passage, where you are invited to publicly claim your identity in the world and step more fully into your power. If you hurt during this process, if you cry, if you scream and throw your hands up in the air and say, "I'm giving up!" and then return again the next day to keep trying: you are doing it right. Let it be joyful, let it be painful, let it be everything that crossing a threshold entails.

Networking, Otherwise Known as Engaging in Community

A referral network is all the people who may *refer to you* and who *you refer to*. Those people are not always the same; there may be people who refer to you who you do not refer back to or vice versa. Much can be said about "successful networking," but the single-most-important thing to remember about it is that *it is the simple human act of maintaining meaningful connection to other human beings.* You can do this in person or online. In person, people often find others to build professional relationships with through consultation groups, classes, conferences, professional associations, and other community-based meetings. Online, people do this through all the ways previously listed, though on an online platform such as social media and email lists. Making a referral is a serious endeavor. As healing practitioners we mostly refer to people we know and trust. Sometimes we make referrals to people we do not know, but when we do that we cannot make as strong of a referral, because we cannot speak to the trust we have in their skills.

People with very strong referral networks build *real, meaningful relationships.* Picture this: you meet a fellow healer at a conference, chat for fifteen minutes, and give them your card. You are really hoping this person will refer clients to you. That same person is in a consultation group or a study group that meets every other week, where they hear about the other healers' practices. They learn about what these other practitioners' strengths are, what their passions are, and truly what their sacred purpose is. They build a sense of trust, knowing that they could feel solid about sending people to their colleagues for support. They get a referral they cannot take that would be a perfect fit for you, but they don't give your name, because they have completely forgotten about that fifteen-minute chat and it doesn't hold up in comparison to the deep relationships they have built with several other clinicians. If you choose to communicate your sacred intentions to the world through community, part of your job will be building very meaningful relationships with other healers. You can study together, consult together, do projects together, team up to do events, or just meet for coffee regularly. This way they actually truly know your work and trust you, and are thus far more likely to refer to you. Just sending one email or meeting up once for coffee means you need to make an incredible impression to get referrals, which is a tall order for most people.

People with strong referral networks connect with healing practitioners who do the same work as they do. And I mean down to networking with people who have the exact same specialties and modalities. Many healers don't want to do this. It is easy to feel competitive and imagine that you should connect only with healers who do something different, because of course you will be the one offering astrology and they will be the one who offers breathwork, and it will never feel uncomfortable or competitive. But the reality is that close relationships require us to feel tons of emotions that are uncomfortable. Intimacy isn't permanent joy. It is the ongoing complexity of loving and staying close to someone through hardship and ease. That competitive approach to building a professional community is based in fear. These people are your peers, not your competition. And if you feel so much animosity toward someone who does similar work as you and is successful at it—it is time to explore why that bothers you. Are you not attempting to be successful in your path too? It is normal to struggle with comparison or feel envy; it is part of desiring something you don't have yet. It doesn't have to be a harmful thing to want more out of life. Under the right circumstances, it can even be inspiring. It is helpful to have a referral network of similar practitioners. There are a lot of reasons someone will refer to you: a client has called them and their schedules don't match, a client has called them and there is too much social overlap for them to work together, a client has called and it just isn't a good fit, but they want someone who does similar work. If you do an obscure form of healing, it's even better, because you are joining together to educate the world about your healing so that more people are able to seek it out and access it.

The other very important task in having a strong referral network is to actually make referrals. This is huge. You cannot expect others to be on their game, referring left and right, if you aren't also on your game. Almost every time someone tells me they need professional support, I offer them names of potential matches or I offer my email or my number for them to contact me later. I have helped everyone from best friends, to neighbors, to people I have randomly met at a party to find a healing practitioner. Every time I have a good experience with a healer, I refer people to them. I have my favorite astrologers, intuitives, tarot readers, and so on. I love helping people find a healing relationship. You may be wondering why this is helpful to you. Well, first of all, you need to be the world you want to live in, not just expect others to be it. So, if you want twenty referrals this year, commit yourself to making twenty referrals to others. Second, most healing practitioners will ask how a potential client got their information (and if you aren't doing this, start now). When someone says, Laura Northrup gave me your number, I am staying on that healer's radar. I am letting them know: I am still here and I am engaged in the profession. Sometimes before I refer to someone, I will ask them if they have space. That lets them know that I am thinking about them, and it says: *you are in my referral network.* When someone refers to you, send them a thank you. You don't need to say, "Thank you for sending Georgia my way. She's a delight to work with"; that is not respectful of your client's privacy. You can just say, "Thanks for thinking of me for referrals." This gratitude goes a long way and shows that you understand the collective orientation and mutual care that it takes to survive in this world. Even though you might be in what is commonly referred to as "private practice" or a "sole proprietorship," you are in a community that mutually sustains life. One final note on making referrals: don't refer to people you don't actually trust or believe in. As a healer you are centering truth and integrity. Yes, referring to people can mean they will in turn refer to you. But that is not *why* we make referrals and it is not a spiritually grounded reason to refer to someone. We refer people to practitioners so they can heal, not so that we can get in good favor with another practitioner. This doesn't mean you cannot refer to people you do not know; we have to do that all the time. But it does mean you can be honest and say, "I don't know this person, but they have space open for new people."

Online networking is similar in many ways, and I think it is very useful to be part of a few email lists or social media groups. These groups broaden your referral base and they provide you with opportunities to learn about new things and connect with new people. For example, maybe you need to refer someone to a birth doula, but you don't actually know any birth doulas. Or your client asks you for advice about finding someone in another state where you don't know anyone. As with any of these forms of communicating and connecting with the world, choose something and do it well. So, if you join an email list, really consider which one will work best for you and commit to actually engaging with it and using it, rather than joining fifteen different ones and ignoring them because of the onslaught of forty additional emails per day.

Communicating through Word of Mouth

Word of mouth is similar to a referral network, but it is more passive and also includes people you currently or formerly worked with, as well as people who are not clinicians of any kind. This style of communicating with the world requires a lot of connection to community, because you need to be known by many people. It is an excellent way to build a practice; however, similar to a referral network, it takes years to make it very strong. If this is the primary way you wish to connect with the people you serve, just know that it may take time to build your practice. Though once you do, it will mean that you have many people who trust you and refer to you. If you live in a small town and don't do any remote work, this can be an easier way to grow your practice than in a saturated area.

Communicating through Free Offerings

Free offerings are a great way to get your name out there with little risk to the people you want to serve. This could be a blog, a podcast, being a guest on someone else's podcast, an event, a class, a free handout on your website, or even just posts on social media. A very important aspect of offering something free is that it has to be something of value, something that would be worth paying for. If you offer something with no value, you communicate that you offer things with little value. So, for example, perhaps you want to build your email list. You have a free handout on your website that people get when they sign up with their email. Let's say that you are an astrologer and you send out an email once per month. Your free handout and your emails need to be super valuable. They need to demonstrate the breadth of your knowledge, the depth of your beliefs, and they need to have a clear invitation for more in-depth, personalized support through working with you. If you send out emails that are meaningless or basic, or don't show much about what you actually have to offer, it won't work. In fact, it may backfire. I once went to a "free" class where the instructor mostly covered basic materials offered for free online and then did a sales pitch for the majority of the class; I was not inspired to work with that person again or refer people to them. It truly has to be an offering, given without expectation for something in return.

I think of certain free offerings as a labor of love and a service to the world, especially if you are doing in-person events. It is very time intensive to teach a class, and the likelihood that any of the participants will want to work with you really depends on who showed up and how much they connected with you. However, if you love teaching and want to offer this as a service to the world, free of charge, it is a great way to give to others.

Communicating through Advertising

Paid advertising is similar to gambling, and as my Vegas-loving grandmother always said, "Know what you are willing to lose, and stick to that." If you choose some paid advertising, just remember that you can stay connected to your own integrity through the process. You do not have to do anything that doesn't sit right with you spiritually or emotionally. There is also "free" advertising, if you consider things like having an active social media account or listing yourself on directories as a form of advertising. Though most of those platforms also have a paid version. You do not need to do paid advertising to have a successful practice, but if you would like to do it, it can be a helpful way to find clients. There are two ways I recommend making decisions about paid advertising:

1. Ask yourself how many sessions of your work you will have to do to simply cover the cost of the paid advertising. Now ask yourself: do you think you could reasonably get *at least* that many sessions from this ad? If so, it's worth the risk. If you do the math and it seems possible you would risk not even covering the cost, then you may as well pass. Trying and breaking even is the minimum where I set the bar.

2. Back to Grandma's wisdom: how much are you willing to spend on trying something and have it not work? If you have been to a casino, you know that it's likely you will lose money. So, even though you want to win money, you have to ask yourself how much you would feel *comfortable* losing, and don't go over that amount. I have seen healers go over that amount and have nothing in return and be financially wrecked for months. If a marketing agency tries to swindle you or tells you they will fill your practice for a hefty price, really consider what they are actually guaranteeing and what your risks are. Most credible paid advertising has smaller fee options and larger fee options so that you can dip your toe in the water without drowning.

Remember that whatever you choose, you will be doing it for a long time. It takes years to become highly skilled at knowing one's self, articulating one's needs and offerings to the world, and developing the ability to do it with a particular method such as the ones described above. The essence of what you offer and why you offer it needs to be imbued in every aspect of your communication with the world, making it essential that you really do the work to listen to yourself and let the things that are unique about you shine through and be a part of the medicine that you offer. If you try to mimic what other healers are doing, do what someone told you is the "best" way to grow your practice even if you despise it, or generally aren't being yourself—you won't connect with the people you have dedicated your path to, and you will be drained rather than energized. If you are in this for the long haul, you need to truly develop your practice around who you are.

EXERCISES AND EXPERIENTIALS
CHAPTER 8

8.1 *Reflection*

1. How did you feel reading this chapter? What did you notice in your body?

2. Did any of the methods of communication immediately stand out to you as ones you would strongly dislike?

3. Which one of these methods of communication are you most drawn to?

8.2 *Writing*

1. Which type of communication most suits your personality and the type of community you enjoy building? Why?

2. What fears come up when you consider committing to one of these forms of communication?

3. What feels exciting about trying one out?

8.3 *Research*

Choose a method and start researching. That could mean you try building a website, it could mean you look into existing email lists to join, or it could even mean you try designing a free class you might teach.

8.4 *Connection*

Colleagueship is very important in the general healing field, even if you don't end up building your practice through a strong referral network. Who are your current colleagues? Make a time to connect with someone you either already have a relationship with and would like to deepen or someone new.

Accessing Spirit

Intentions, Rituals, and Rites of Passage

Connecting to Spirit

Spirituality can get fairly twisted here in the United States. In popular culture, meditation has become a five-minute practice using an app that rewards us points for each session, with goals such as reduction of stress to increase productivity at work. In the psychedelic realm, medicine guides are being replaced with "trip sitting" apps to assist with deep spiritual transformation. A far cry from the teachings of the Buddha or María Sabina, this is the result of colonization and being a "super" power: being encouraged to be *super* alienated from our own humanity.

If you already have a spiritual practice and/or a strong relationship with your ancestors, you can use your existing rituals and connections to ask for support and guidance in sustaining your path. The examples and suggestions I give here may resonate or they may need to be modified to fit your existing practice. I encourage you to follow your intuition and do whatever makes the most sense to you. If you are embedded in a spiritual community, the elders or peers may be other sources of guidance and wisdom to call upon in developing practices to support your path.

If you are a person who does not have a spiritual practice, it can be hard to even understand what connection to spirit can offer or why it might be important in supporting your developing path. First of all, it can help hold your work on a daily and lifelong basis. At times, working with sexual trauma, one of my areas of focus, can be emotionally unbearable. When I first started practicing, I didn't understand that, and I suffered immensely holding so much violence and pain on my own. However, with the help of my therapist, spiritual guidance from others, and plant medicines, I have come to understand that there is no single person who can hold and heal the incomprehensible level of violence humanity is capable of, all by themselves. Every day I am supported by the fact that something much larger than me holds the healing work that I do. I am not alone; I am part of a much larger web. I am not facing my client's pain alone, even if I am visibly the only one listening, because I have the assistance of Earth and spirit. When I feel overwhelmed, I know how to get connected to that larger force.

Second, it can help to guide you. My connection to spirit is part of what helps me stay connected to my truth and in integrity. Connecting to your ancestors or to some form of spiritual source also connects you to your values and helps to guide you and keep you on track throughout your life. The simple practice of taking time each day to feel into what matters most to you is a spiritual practice.

Regardless of what individual people or religions may teach: there are many ways to be spiritual, and that is a beautiful thing. Your creativity and agency are welcome in connecting to spirit. The following are a few practices that may help you.

Intention-Setting

I have talked about intention quite a bit so far, because it is foundational to a spiritual practice and it creates a solid base for your healing practice to flourish. A key thing to remember about intentions is that they exist, regardless of whether we think about them or not. So rather than let unconscious intentions run your life, it is essential to unearth what already exists and to consciously hone them. If one of your unconscious intentions is to prove to yourself that your inner critic is right and that everything you try fails— welcome to a failing practice. Intentions are powerful tools that guide us and help us to manifest our goals. In a nutshell, setting intentions is the spiritual process of bringing energy to a task and manifesting it. When you determine an intention or a prayer of some sort, you have to engage with it regularly. As in the example above about having an inner critic: most people engage their inner critics quite regularly, with some people speaking the prayer of self-criticism all day long. You need to be engaging your conscious intentions with as much rigor. Through a daily spiritual engagement with a task, you refine it and it grows. Spiritually speaking, you are in a process of devoting yourself to that intention or prayer.

There are many ways people work with intentions and prayers. For those who are new to spiritual practice or want to expand their existing one, I am going to lay out a basic structure for you to start with. You can consciously work with intentions for any aspect of your practice. It could be your intention to discern what your next step is on your path, it could be about how you want to deepen the work you are already doing, or it could even be about how you want to show up to a healing relationship with a single person in your practice. Intentions can be made for anything. Once you have a sense of something you would like to work on, you can write down your intention or prayer. Writing it down is helpful in engaging with it in a concrete and defined way. It can be as long or as short as you want. My only suggestion is to make it meaningful and to hone it. If it feels vague, partially articulated, or it floats on a shallow surface—it is not done and you can continue to craft it. Just because you wrote it down doesn't mean that you cannot rewrite it and let it evolve over time. Everything in life is in progress, despite what we tell ourselves, and your intentions get to change and grow as you grow. After you have the written document of your intentions, you can set aside time to give it attention on a daily basis through speaking it aloud or reading it to yourself, mindfully. Mindful reading means you are not doing it while you drive, or while you watch television. It means you are devoting all of your attention to it, in an unrushed manner. There is a lot of magic in doing this process, especially when done in an embodied way.

So, for a more specific example, I will use something that I actually did in relationship to a project that I worked on. I made a podcast series called *Inside Eyes* that defines sexual violence as a form of spiritual abuse and explores the use of entheogens and psychedelics in the healing process. It includes several personal interviews with people who are survivors of sexual violence who have used entheogens or psychedelics to heal their trauma. This series was very important to me and took an immense amount of work. I easily spent five hundred hours in the creation of it. Early on in my process I told several people about it. Some people responded that they thought it would not have many listeners because it was so niche. I felt discouraged. Some people said I should just work to make it entertaining, so that even people who aren't survivors of sexual violence would want to listen. For a short period, I felt caught in a dilemma. I was making a serious audio series, *but should I make it more dramatic or more entertaining?* I hadn't even thought about how many people would listen, but I was suddenly feeling inferior and concerned with a large audience size. However, something about that did not feel right to me. Sexual violence is not a form of entertainment, despite what the film industry may think. My truest intention in creating the series was to help people, not boost my own ego with a large listener base. This type of feedback was regular enough that it chipped away at my self-confidence and my true intentions in making the series. So I wrote out my intentions. I made them very simple so that I could read them easily, every day. They were something along the lines of:

> *I am making this series for survivors. When I am done it will be a success if even one person finds it helpful.*

I wrote this down on a piece of paper and hung it over the area where I sat for more than three hundred hours editing the series. Every time I questioned what I was doing, I had that intention right there to ground me. Whenever I felt scared or tired or worried that my efforts were pointless, those words guided me. And obviously, I did a lot of work to make sure more than one person heard the series, because that is a part of helping people. But the point of my intentions was to redirect myself to what really mattered: that I was called to do this regardless of how much it personally benefited me; that centering healing and vital information was the focus, not entertainment;

and that I would be staying in my own integrity regardless of what feedback I was given or what directions people suggested I go in. I read that intention to myself every day for months. It was through that process that I was able to make the series.

By crafting an intention and spending meaningful time with it every day, you are devoting yourself to it. Through time you will know: Is this prayer something you want to devote yourself to, or was it just a fleeting interest? Do you continue to believe in it and feel inspired by it? Do you see ways that it needs to be different? The big work comes in realizing what may need to change in the concrete, external world in order to make this prayer come to fruition. For example, if you want to have a thriving healing practice and you haven't found an office location yet, an early step in manifesting this prayer will be finding the container for it.

Many people find this process to be too "woo woo" or "new age" and are turned off by the idea of praying or doing ritual intention-setting, due to religious trauma. I want you to think about a job that you had where you worked for someone else, or a sports team you played on, or anything where you were in a group setting and you joined someone else's vision that you participated in, but were not the sole creator of. If you think back to that time, everything you did was in service of a value and an intention, and there were likely daily tasks associated with manifesting that. The ritual of morning meetings, the ritual of running a track, the ritual of practicing plays, or doing rehearsal run-throughs, or even the ritual of your lunch break—all these things are the daily rituals required to manifest the prayer of that company or collective group. Full company meetings are the ritual of recommitting to a task, detailing how each part of the group will help to manifest the vision. However, in capitalist-driven work environments, the intention underlying it all is often to make as much money as possible, regardless of how that impacts the most vulnerable people. It is possible that if you were not the boss or company owner, you would have been participating in the rituals, but your opinion on the intentions or manifestation process would be less considered. Over time, being on a team and going through the daily tasks of these devotional rituals allows you to get more clear on what parts you believe in and what parts you wish were different. This discernment that emerges through repetition and devotion is pure wisdom. In working for yourself as a healer, you alone will be creating many of these rituals. You have the power to devote yourself to a higher calling and refine that calling and the process by which it will be achieved, through spending intentional time in consideration of it. This isn't new to you, though it may be new to be the sole creator of it or to think of it as a spiritual act.

If it resonates with you, you can also create an altar to do this work at. An altar is an intentional space for you to practice your intentions or prayers, and to show reverence for any entity or thing that you receive teachings or guidance from. It typically includes items that connect you to those entities or things that support you—these could be items that bring the energy of your ancestors, your living loved ones, mentors, the spirits of nonhuman entities such as plants, or items that inspire you, such as poems, songs, or other forms of art.

Cosmic Pizza Order

This next practice comes from a dear friend and fellow psychotherapist, Eugenia Guidi. Manifestation rituals are fairly self-explanatory: you are trying to manifest something into the concrete realm that is currently just a dream. Although I had been doing manifestation rituals for some years, Eugenia introduced me to what she calls the Cosmic Pizza Order,[7] and what I love about this one is the level of detail. Just like when you order a pizza, you get to be very specific about each of the toppings. For this practice you will write out your intentions again; however, you write everything out as though it has already happened, in great detail. You can work with it daily or at least a few times per week—the level of energy you put in is correlated with what you get out of it. If you do a manifestation ritual for your practice, be sure to include what you are offering in addition to what you hope to receive. For example, rather than saying, "I have a thriving practice," one could say, "I have a thriving practice as an end-of-life doula, where I support people who are dying and their families in a meaningful engagement with death through a wise and loving presence. The people I serve die with dignity, and their families receive profound healing from the process." The Cosmic Pizza Order is set with a clear and detailed vision of the outcome: how they will feel, how you will feel, and as many details as you can muster. While intention-setting is often about honing-in and condensing what you want to say into one or two sentences, this method is far more detailed.

After working for months with my basic intention-setting that I previously described, I decided to shift and do a daily manifestation ritual for the podcast à la the Cosmic Pizza Order. The work was intense: I was still working full time in my clinical practice while editing interviews on the weekends about a very intense and emotionally evocative topic. The spiritual work that I did during that time increased my capacity to manage the workload. Making the series also required me to do an immense amount of personal healing work. It took a lot of self-confidence and touched on many wounds as I made it. At some point I drew on the teachings of Spring Washam, a Buddhist meditation teacher, who once told me to think of myself as though I was in a spiritual hospital (this was at another time in my life when I was doing a big piece of healing work). She talked about how when someone is in the hospital, they need to be mindful of who they are around and what they do, because they are healing and vulnerable. This was essential advice. Additionally, I had come to view my editing space and the general space I occupied during the making of the podcast as my spiritual laboratory: "spirit lab" for short. In creating my intention, I also decided to include the desire to get the show out to many people. While I was still reminding myself that even if one single person benefited from it the effort was worth it, I was clear that I wanted everyone who could benefit to have the knowledge of its existence. It might seem materialistic or egoic to focus on the numbers, but the material world is real and it is perfectly spiritually grounded to have an intention to support many people. I wrote out my Cosmic Pizza Order as follows:

I am in spirit hospital and spirit lab, both of which I need in order to create and birth this prayer. My prayer emerges healthy, vibrant, and powerful— fulfilling its highest purpose of service to this world. This series is for survivors of sexual violence. It is not a form of entertainment; it is in service of collective healing. Thousands of people listen to Inside Eyes and become more conscious and act on creating a just world. I have finished the season, survivors find it helpful, and I thrive and am satisfied with its release.

And that is exactly what happened. I released the podcast and received many emails from listeners who said it was a guiding light for them. Many people said it inspired them to think differently about sexual violence, now understanding the political and spiritual significance of it. Thousands of people listened and I managed to stay in full integrity with how I wanted the series to be. Devoting yourself to such a detailed description of what will occur is a compass that guides you through every decision you make, every step of the way. And of course, magic makes it happen too.

Intention-Setting with Others

Intention-setting doesn't have to be a solitary practice, and there can be unique power and healing in doing this work with others. By telling other people about your intentions, you enlist them on your team as supports, and you benefit from one another's magic. It is also an act of confronting any shame that may surround your intentions. Shame is an emotion that makes us feel disconnected and afraid to be revealed to others. By sharing your intentions and experiencing support rather than judgment from others, you get to have a reparative experience.

Group rituals can take on many forms, and once you have found others to practice with, you can design rituals however you please. However, building from the rituals previously described, here is a simple way of doing a group ritual: Each of you can write out your intentions and give each other copies. Much as you would practice each day with just your own ritual, each participant can take the copies home and put them (one of everyone else's intentions plus their own) on an altar or some other type of sacred space set aside for this purpose. What you do at the altar can be determined by you; it could be as simple as reading everyone's intentions aloud each day for a set amount of days or lighting a candle for them. Whatever you choose, the point is to do it mindfully and with focus. If you do a group ritual that extends into days of self-practice with everyone's intentions, I suggest starting it out with a more structured ritual to punctuate opening the space for this work. In turn, you can do some form of closing when it is done.

Rituals can get complex and include the sacred use of plants, the sacred use of fire (candles), and/or calling in spirits, ancestors, and deities. If you have never done any ritual, engaging in a group process with more experienced ritualists can be a nice way to learn.

Remember to be discerning when choosing people. You are entrusting the people in your ritual to carry a very important part of your process with you. Doing this with someone who does not have your best intentions in mind (either consciously or unconsciously) is not spiritually or energetically safe. For example, someone may envy you and secretly hope you do not succeed, or perhaps someone doesn't totally believe in you and privately dismisses your hopes, or perhaps desires to be cared for by you beyond what you've agreed upon (and is thus draining). This is not a good dynamic to be in. If you find yourself being the one who feels dismissive, envious, longing to be parented, or any other type of unsupportive feelings—excuse yourself from the ritual. It is not useful to you or to the other person or people to engage in spiritual work that is unkind or a misuse of the other participants.

On Compulsive Rituals

You may have noticed I sometimes talk about "rituals" of behavior, such as the ritual of compulsive research. And you might be wondering why I would use this term, considering that ritual is also a sacred way of creating space to connect to the divine or to hold a healing space. I believe that ritualized behavior such as compulsively researching or repeating an action is an attempt at creating that spiritual space; however, something is limiting the ritual so that its full potential and purpose are cut short. Repeatedly creating a financial budget when you already have a working one might be an attempt to ritually process underlying fears that will never be soothed by a financial budget, but rather need to be addressed on a far-deeper level. We can get stuck in unsuccessful rituals, especially private ones that don't include the help of other people or spirit. This comes from living in an increasingly isolating dominant culture that doesn't normalize deeper spiritual transformation or community-level holding. If you get stuck in compulsive rituals that don't resolve, consider seeking out healing support to move through them in a different way. Ritual work is a normal part of being human, and your ancestors did it for thousands of years. Even if your current generation is disconnected from it, with only disorganized echoes remaining, you can reconnect; it comes naturally to many people.

Working with Self-Compassion and Self-Love

In addition to her idea of a spiritual hospital, Spring Washam is also the person who introduced me to *mettā* meditation, a Buddhist loving-kindness practice. You know how people often suggest meditation, and if you have never done it, you might sort of look back at them and think: *Sure ... that could help, but I'm not going to do it ... it is too much work.* I was an infrequent meditator at the time—I valued it without prioritizing it. However, when Spring suggested that I do mettā every day, it was as if the sky parted and a single beam of light shot through the dense part of me that previously rejected the idea of committing myself to daily meditation. Spring is very loving, and she delivered these instructions in the kindest, most gentle manner, but my mind translated it to: "Do you want to sit around and complain about your suffering, or do you actually want to heal, because this is it right here—*you can love yourself.*" This is all to say, mettā meditation is an excellent way to work with self-compassion and self-love, or conversely to overcome self-criticism and self-hatred. It is also a practice for cultivating loving-kindness toward others, which is essential in the path of healership. If you struggle with compassion and love for yourself, you will struggle to build a healing practice. It takes a lot of love to realize your dreams. I am not going to explain mettā practice here, only suggest it, because there are many Buddhist practitioners who are far more skilled than I, who already have.

When Spring told me to do mettā meditation, she told me that if I couldn't do it for myself, that I should get a picture of myself as a baby, because it is sometimes easier to feel compassion for baby-you. I was sobbing and staring at a baby photo within twenty-four hours. So, here is one last solo ritual I suggest, which is modified from doing mettā, but was originally inspired by the wisdom of Spring and the Buddha. It is more focused on connecting to the medicine within you and healing younger versions of yourself in service of your path.

Get a photo of yourself as a baby, and if you don't have one you can write your name on a piece of paper and something that indicates you are conjuring a baby version of you (e.g., "Baby [Your Name]"). Make a pleasant space to sit with the photo or name on paper where you will not be interrupted. If you already have an altar, that is a great spot to do this. Let yourself get settled and as embodied as is accessible to you. Now take a look at this image or these words. This is you. It is you when you were innocent, at a time when all you were was the living prayer and hope of all your ancestors. It is hard to judge a baby. This is you when the medicine inside of you was raw and young, a whisper waiting to become a song. Be curious: What was your medicine like then? What gifts did you come into this world with? Imagine how you would treat the baby version of yourself. Would you berate baby-you? Would you criticize baby-you for not working hard enough? Would you shame baby-you for understandable mistakes? Would you neglect baby-you by ignoring your needs and the needs of your path? It's hard to treat a baby poorly. Remember that although you are an adult, you are also a vulnerable person who was once a baby. While you have more responsibilities now, you are still a human being who needs respect and love to function. If you were not treated well as a baby or as a child (or at any other time in your life), let yourself grieve the lack of love. Let yourself know on the deepest level that it has never been okay for anyone to harm you, and you do not have to continue to harm yourself. While you are keeping baby-you in mind, feel free to ask if there is anything the younger versions of yourself need in order for you to keep moving on your path. Sometimes wounded parts of us can significantly hold us back and need some form of attention to be soothed and join in the efforts toward your future. You may hear a response from younger-you as a voice, but be open—it may also come as a sensation, an image, an impulse, or a simple awareness. If you get a response, remember that it is now your job to tend to this part. To neglect the need is to further the wound; to tend to it is to heal. Close your ritual baby connection in whatever way feels meaningful; it could be as simple as thanking baby-you for the time and committing yourself to the next step in the work. You can return to this ritual as many times as you need, especially if the communication with this part of you is slower and requires several visits.

Sometimes with rituals like this, people say to me, "Laura, I start crying and I cannot stop! I think there is something wrong with me." They do eventually stop, but I understand that it can be unsettling to cry for a long period of time. My response is, "There is a lot of crying and grieving to do." Trust your own body. If you need to cry for an hour, then do it. It is meaningful. If you need to cry every day for an entire year, then do it. You are doing something powerful and it has a purpose. Crying may be the very thing the younger-you needs in order to heal and comfortably join you on your current path.

Sometimes compassion is equated with not trying hard or not being pushed to do things, but I do not adhere to that use of the word. If you are neglecting the work of building your practice, that is not actually compassionate. A part of you wants to thrive, and you know it. Self-compassion is about kindness. And it is kind to make sure you do the things that will make this a fulfilling life. You don't need to be mean to yourself and overwork or expect your practice to hit unreasonable goals. But you also don't need to ignore it or not expect much out of yourself.

You can do this ritual as I just described or add much more. You could build an altar for the baby-you, build an altar to self-compassion, create a music playlist for your inner child, or create a self-love playlist; you could sing songs to baby-you, or have a chat with your inner kid, or write intentions for self-compassion and ritually commit to them—the sky is the limit. Creating ritual is about making a space for deep presence and connection. It is a process of stepping out of the everyday and into a very intentional and magical state. You can design that in whatever way allows you to access that state.

Altars, Containment, and Frequency of Practice

People access spirit in many different ways, and creating a regular and deep practice makes it easier. Like most things, this type of work is a skill. Much like learning to play an instrument, it takes many hours of practice to create something satisfying to the ears and the soul. If you try it once, or do it rarely, your skill level will reflect that. Accessing spirit has many purposes; and in the context of your path, it is a great way to feel the support of your ancestors and whatever spiritual deities you believe in, as well as connect to your deepest truths as a guiding force. Just as with any relationship in your life, it can be hard to keep it fresh, alive, and meaningful if contact is infrequent or inconsistent. People who are new to this work or have never felt the support of ancestors or other spirit forces may be asking, "What's the point?" And to that I would say: while this path is not for everyone, keep an open mind. It is possible that a level of support you never imagined was attainable is available, and it might radically transform your life. However, you have to be open to it to find out.

Intention-setting or connecting to spirit is not just a verbal or mental practice; it helps to deepen your work by creating a meaningful *physical* space to practice in. For this I recommend creating an altar. You can create a general altar for all your spiritual work, or you can create a specific altar for a specific spiritual task (e.g., an altar to support your healing practice or an altar to heal childhood wounds). Not everyone has the wealth privilege to access ample indoor space, personal space, or private outdoor space. Additionally, not everyone has access to a space where it is safe to have a spiritual practice. If you feel uncomfortable practicing spirituality in your home or you do not have any physical space to do it, you can create an altar in other ways. I am a fan of what I call the "pocket altar" or the "portable altar," which is items small enough to put in one pocket and set up an altar anywhere. If there is a park or other public space that you can access, it is possible to make a pack of items that is a transportable altar (it doesn't have to all fit in your pocket). A certain tree that you visit every day could be your altar. With a little creativity, spiritual space is always accessible, regardless of your class or financial access.

Ritual space needs containment. The better the container, the deeper the work. In short, a container is sort of like the overall effect of the emotional, physical, and spiritual boundaries around an event or space. Strong containment allows for big expansion. Sex is a great example of the containment-expansion phenomenon. For many people, having some privacy with a sexual partner (containment) allows for greater sexual freedom (expansion). Alternatively, if you were staying with your parents or extended family, for example, you may not feel as comfortable having loud sex (contraction), because they may hear you (lack of containment) and you don't want them included. Containment inside can include closing doors, noting who is around or has access to the space, and being clear about what spirits are welcome.

It is possible to create containment outside or in public. If you go out to coffee with a friend and sit at a two-person table together, the table is part of what creates the container. There are only two chairs at it and only two of you, and that creates a certain level of intimacy. Of course, the intimacy will reflect both of your comfort levels and it will reflect the fact that you are in public (people nearby could hear you or start up conversation with you). If you are practicing outdoors due to lack of access to indoor space or because the outdoors is required for your practice, creating containment could be as simple as emitting a vibe that says to strangers: do not interrupt this. You can also make the boundaries of the container through movement, by delineating it with a physical marking (e.g., drawing in the sand if you are on the beach), having a mat or other item that you bring to show the space/boundary, through the burning of herbs, or even by the simple spoken statement: "I am making a container here now. I invite any unhelpful energies to leave." Certainly, there are some rituals that cannot be completed in a public space, so use your judgment about what level of safety and protection is needed before starting the ritual.

And finally, caring for the container includes cleaning it before and after use. Just like you don't want to sit at a dirty table in a café, or come to therapy and see the tissues from the last client strewn on the couch, you want to clear any space of whatever it was used for previously and clean up (contain) after your ritual. If you are using your own space it might be tempting not to clean, because no one else is entering the space. However, even you can expose yourself to your own mess. If you neglect to clean you are practicing in a neglected container—which has an energetic impact.

Accessing Spirit in an Altered State

One method of connecting to spirit is through altered-state work. Altered-state work is a great place to do a deeper dive into spiritual connection, which can then be a resource to keep returning back to in your daily life.

Altered-state work includes meditation, prayer, trance, breathwork, ancestral reverence work, psychedelics, entheogenic plant medicine work, and any other practice that takes you out of your normal waking realm and into a strong direct connection with spirit.

If you have an existing relationship to altered-state work, you can draw on it as-is to support you in your path, or you may choose to deepen it at this time. For example, if you meditate daily, consider doing a longer residential retreat. If you have no existing relationship to altered-state work, take a class or find some manner in which to be supported by someone with more knowledge. Working in an altered-state realm is not easy, and I do not recommend anyone attempt it without proper guidance. Remember that what works for others may not work for you, so do not be discouraged if you have to explore multiple methods or have multiple mentors before landing on the one that most resonates with you.

If you are a trauma survivor, be mindful that altered-state work can be evocative. Often, trauma survivors are taken by surprise at how intense it can be to enter an altered state, because unhealed trauma can start to emerge in the form of painful memories, discomfort in the body, and fragmented or tormented thinking. Fortunately, there are many types of altered-state work and many degrees of intensity. Meditating for three minutes is very different from eating nine grams of psilocybin-containing mushrooms. With any method you choose, you can start small and build up to what makes the most sense for you. I am specifically advocating that you keep in mind *what makes the most sense for you,* rather than falling into the idealization of intense experiences, such as high-dose entheogen work or months of meditation retreat. You do not need to pursue the most intense experience available in order to be spiritually connected or evolved. There is a lot of power in subtle work and there is immense power in slow work. Many people seek out intense experiences as though they are performing deep work, while they neglect the very simple and slow work of mindfully being in loving connection with people in their lives. Often, complete ego dissolution or reaching a state of oneness with all life are revered as the ultimate goals of altered-state work. Not everyone needs to experience ego dissolution to be on their spiritual path. If you have experienced ego dissolution or seen someone experience it, you know that it can be terrifying and incomprehensibly uncomfortable. For trauma survivors who have endured substantial attack on their egos, this process can be harming if it is done without care or at the wrong time. When in doubt listen to yourself and go slow. The point is not to re-traumatize yourself or have an experience that makes an exciting story for others. The point is to deepen your connection to your spirituality and let it inform your path.

Rites of Passage

In many cultures some type of ceremonial rite of passage marks big life transitions and the crossing of thresholds. Stepping into your path as a healer is one of those thresholds. In the dominant culture of the United States, ceremonial practices are less valued and often replaced with ritual events that don't explicitly connect us to spirit. I think about some of the events marking the transition out of my graduate school experience and into the practicing of my craft. One of them was very impersonal: a massive, boring graduation ceremony with more than a thousand people I didn't know, including a speaker I had never heard of. Another was entirely focused on government approval: passing my marriage and family therapist exams through a grueling six hours of tests in isolation on a computer, in a basement office in the suburbs, only to emerge victorious to a massive parking lot, alone. And some were mostly about capitalist competency: for example, the rite of passage that comes with being able to afford rent and secure one's own office in a cutthroat rental market. While each of these was an important marker, they felt devoid of community witnessing and spiritually misattuned to what was actually happening.

Crossing thresholds and honoring them is important. Depending on the healing tradition you work within and your culture of origin, you may have meaningful rites of passage or you may experience more of the cultural neglect I just described. Whichever the case, I encourage you to find a way to honor big transitions in your path in an attuned manner. A rite of passage typically includes witnessing from community and a formal acknowledgment of your shifting role. There are many ways to make that happen if it is not already available to you.

Rites of passage are a normal part of being human, and while they may or may not be a recent memory in your individual mind, they are something that our collective humanity intimately knows. Much as with unconscious compulsive rituals, you are likely engaging in some form of process around rites of passage regardless of your conscious intention to do them. With all things that occur unconsciously, there is the question: can you bring more consciousness, meaning, and purpose to it?

EXERCISES AND EXPERIENTIALS
CHAPTER 9

9.1 *Writing*

1. How do you feel about spirituality, and where do your beliefs come from?

2. Are there ways you would like to be more spiritual or ways you would like your spirituality to be different?

3. How do you typically mark big moments and thresholds?

4. How have elders or mentors helped to shepherd you through rites of passage in the past?

5. What are ways you may want to honor crossing thresholds differently in the future?

6. How could your existing spiritual practice, or the creation of one, specifically support you in sustaining your practice?

9.2 *Research*

What is the next step for you in regards to rituals, intentions, and rites of passage? Do you need mentorship? Do you need to learn more? Do some research, starting with where your current interests exist. Books, elders, spiritual mentors, and classes are great ways to further your study and growth in these realms.

9.3 *Practice*

Choose one of the exercises within the chapter or create your own and try it out. Setting intentions and creating rituals can seem daunting, but don't let it get too precious. Have fun, experiment, and make it meaningful for you.

9.4 Resources

If you would like to learn more about mettā meditation, there are many books and talks on the topic. I recommend Spring Washam's book *A Fierce Heart* and Bhante Gunaratana's book *8 Mindful Steps to Happiness*.

10

New Healing Relationships

Some healing practitioners work diligently on everything I have outlined thus far in the book and yet, they cannot get healing relationships off the ground. It could be that many people visit their website, but no one calls. Or they have first sessions, but people seldom return. It could be that they are contacted via phone or email, but then the potential client drops off and nothing comes of it. If you relate to that, this chapter is especially for you. However, the ideas I outline here are useful to anyone, because I am going to describe an approach to dealing with confusing problems that can emerge when creating new healing relationships.

First Contact

Let's look at what I call "first contact." What do I mean by first contact? I mean however you are first in connection with your potential clients. That could be by phone, by email, in person, over social media, or wherever you interact with people. First impressions are important in our line of work. If you have a lot of first phone calls that don't lead to sessions, or a lot of visits to your website but not a lot of calls, it's time to get curious about what you are communicating in your first impression.

Some common first contact problems are:

- Taking far too long to respond to someone

- Lacking confidence

- Feeling anxious and doing whatever off-putting behavior it is you do when you feel anxious

- Being disorganized around scheduling and communication

Ultimately, when we connect with potential clients, we want to be warm, available, responsive, confident, organized, and giving all the necessary information to make it to the actual session. I know some of these things may seem obvious, but the unconscious is a powerful thing. Let's look at *taking far too long to respond* as an example. In consulting for people who are building a practice, I have been surprised at the wide variety of what people think is an appropriate response time. For example, some practitioners think it's fine to wait a week or longer to return a phone call. If you are waiting that long because your practice is full or you do a form of work that has no urgency attached to it, I can understand why there is such a lag time, though stating on your website that you can take up to a week to return contact is prudent. However, often the people who do this have empty practices and cannot figure out why that is. If someone calls you, and you have very few clients, you should call them back immediately. When I hear that someone is waiting a week or longer to return phone calls, the first thought I have is: *something inside of you doesn't want clients.* You are building real relationships with the people you work with, and whatever unhealed relational issues you have will emerge. For some people that can happen at the moment of first contact.

Regarding not calling people back right away, I have heard a variety of reasons, including "I don't want to seem desperate," "I was too busy," and "I don't look at my phone or email often enough." Looking deeper at each of these statements, we can hear the relational concerns. With the first one, it's obvious. The practitioner is saying they feel embarrassed by how badly they need work, and they get anxiety about behaving in a way that reveals their need to the potential client. Extrapolating further, my guess would be that this practitioner is struggling with confidence and self-esteem. They are not thinking: *I don't have any clients, and so this person is so lucky I have space! I should call them back now!* Someday you will have a full practice, and you will have to disappoint people many times by telling them that you do not have space. You don't need to think of yourself as desperate when you are starting. Instead, you are someone with a lot of room to give, and that is a beautiful thing. Remember that people call you because *they want* to connect.

On to the excuse that the practitioner was *too busy* to respond: that is the oldest avoidant attachment excuse in the book. If you relate to using this excuse, consider that if you need clients you should have the unused time in your schedule. Otherwise, where would you be making the time to see the client? If you do not actually have time in your schedule to see clients, yet you don't have any clients, you have a bigger concern on your hands. If you have the time and are making yourself too busy to call people back, explore why you are doing that. When people call us and we consider working with them, we are in a place of need. We need the work to survive. For some people it is so unbearable to be dependent on others that they completely reject dependency by acting as if they do not need anything. "I don't look at my phone or email often enough" is another avoidant behavior that probably reflects some discomfort with intimacy or dependency. It could be not wanting to depend on others, but it could also be that you are afraid to have clients, because they will depend on you. Whatever the case, in this example I am illustrating that there is always room to explore the deeper emotional meaning behind something that can seem quite innocuous.

Next, let's look at *lacking confidence.* It is hard to start out, and few people have loads of confidence at first. The important thing is that you can manage your lack of confidence. If, in response to lacking confidence, you get on the phone with someone and, because you are afraid, you suggest they work with someone else, that is a problem. If you are struggling with lack of confidence, and you aren't sure what is happening, take a very solid look at what you are doing by writing out the whole interaction in a narrative. If it was a phone call, try to remember it and write it all down. You can either take it to a mentor, ask a colleague to help, or try doing some self-analysis. Your job is to figure out: where did the connection fail? Most of us have common ways we deal with relational anxiety around lacking confidence, and so looking to the way that you are in other relationships can be a guide. Typically, it is not pleasant to look at these things, but it is essential to solving this dilemma. Some people act arrogant or overly confident, others will say something self-deprecating, while others will just project a subtle sense that they really can't engage with what the client is bringing in.

Lacking confidence ties into the next common issue with first contact, which is *off-putting anxious behaviors*. We all have them; you are not alone. When I am very anxious I talk too much, and let me tell you: it is humiliating! I once talked through an entire hour of a first date, to the point that my date said almost nothing. I eventually calmed down and we had an amazing connection. We fell in love, and years later the person told me about how for the first hour of the date they were just thinking: *This person is a nightmare, and I have to get away.* I tell you this story because I want to model that however uncomfortable it is to admit our faults, it is essential that we accept them in order to intervene on them. Unfortunately for some people, it is really hard to hide when they feel anxious. It is normal to feel anxious at first contact, despite your desire to work with someone. New clients are strangers to us—it can be a little nerve-racking to feel the juxtaposition of wanting to connect and not knowing someone at all. Common anxious behaviors are things like: talking too much, talking too fast, not talking at all, not breathing while talking, having a sharp tone or coming off as aggressive, belittling the other person, and being overly gracious. Whatever you do when you are anxious in your regular life is probably what you do when you are anxious in your practitioner role. You can take a similar approach to what I outlined above regarding confidence. The goal is to try to figure out what energy is making the conversation disconnect rather than connect.

Remember that people are coming to you in a state of need. They want to be held by a practitioner who feels solid and able to care for them. Confidence and calm go a long way in communicating your inner strength. A very simple trick if you are struggling with how to talk to someone on the phone, or by email, is to write a script. When you are calm and in a present state, make an intake form or a script for yourself that includes all the things you want to make sure you ask them and things you need to tell them (including the logistics of the first appointment).

If you aren't even getting on the phone or into email communication with people, the next thing I recommend to do is a close inventory of what your outward-facing materials are unconsciously expressing. Again, having a mentor or a colleague look at them is a great way to get feedback. Have someone call your voicemail and listen to the message; have someone go over your website or social media presence. When I first started out, my website was the weirdest color of purple. I thought it was so cool. Then a dear friend and colleague let me know that the font was hard to read and that it sort of felt more like a blog on crocheting doilies than a website for psychotherapy. Harsh feedback, but damn, was I grateful to get it.

If you are not a very *organized* person, minimize methods of contact with people. Don't overwhelm yourself with several ways for someone to contact you. Make it work for you. Choose a form of contact that you are committed to checking regularly and that you can update with a vacation responder. State how long it takes you to return contact. If you take up to a week, but you do not tell them that, they will think you just aren't responding. You can create a deeper sense of relationship and containment by telling them in your voicemail or on your website that it could be up to a week, so they know they will still be hearing from you.

First contact is not just a place for the client to decide if they want to work with you; it is also a place where you get to suss out if you want to work with them. Remember that not every person who calls you will be a good fit. If you do a type of work that involves a weekly ongoing relationship, like therapy or coaching, you can also do some first sessions to determine the fit, and it does not need to be decided at the point of first contact. Over time, you will develop your own sense of what clues indicate that it is a promising fit versus a less-than-optimal one.

First Meeting

After you have successfully made your first contact with someone, you have your first meeting. Some practitioners do a type of work that amounts to only one session, while others do work that happens on a weekly basis. Regardless of what level of frequency or duration you will meet with someone, you are still building a relationship with them. Someone who comes for a single session of astrology may come back to you in a year, or may refer their friends. If you have first meetings, but they seldom result in a long-term connection or additional referrals, then it is time to look at what happens in those first meetings. Similar to first contact, consulting with colleagues and mentors to understand what is amiss is a helpful place to start. Below are some other approaches that go into making a first meeting meaningful.

Do Your Best Work

We all have things that help us do our best work. It could be what you eat for breakfast, taking time to meditate, how much sleep you get the night before, or what kind of office space you work well in—whatever it is, you will need to find that clarity and generate it in your healing practice. Sometimes, being able to do your best work requires very big life changes. For example, it is difficult to hold space for others when you are in a high-conflict romantic relationship or even something as simple as an emotionally draining one. If you are in a relationship that significantly drains you or if you live in a very stressful environment, you may need to make a big change before you will be able to build a sustainable practice. Doing your best work is an essential part of what makes your practice successful, healing to others, and meaningful and sustainable for you.

Build a Real Relationship

In the first meeting, it's important to make a real connection with someone. You don't need to pressure yourself to make a profoundly deep commitment in the first meeting, but you do need to make a real connection. Again, whatever issues you have regarding creating intimacy with other people will come out in the creation of healing relationships. For people who work in physical health or a form of medical healing, remember that "bedside manner" is such an important part of healing. Even though you may not be addressing emotional wounds, making a real connection with someone is integral to building a trusting relationship. For people who work in psychological or spiritual healing modalities, a common mistake in trying to make a connection is to feel that you need to go super deep or show the person your skills right away, but that can overwhelm someone. Offering too many resources or attempting to get someone to feel deep emotions, when there is not enough containment yet, creates a sense of misattunement. If you are a healer who works more long term, in the first session you are giving a taste of the depth you are capable of. For medical healers, that doesn't mean you would avoid a diagnosis or not prescribe necessary medicine; however, it does mean that you would approach the emotional aspect of the physical healing with the awareness that full trust has not yet been built. Think about meeting a new colleague or friend: you want to connect, but you aren't going to invade them or say things that make the person feel overly exposed. Many healing practitioners can see a lot about someone as soon as the person starts talking. Perhaps you could make some pretty strong guesses about their defenses, their wounds, their ancestral traumas, what lifestyle choices are contributing to physical health issues—but rather than pointing all that out, make *some gentle, but meaningful* contact with the person and their story. If you are an astrologer, or a person whose healing modality is understood to revolve more around one-time, deep-dive sessions rather than ongoing processing, the scenario is different, but you still want to be mindful about tracking how the client is taking in the information and how overwhelmed or not they seem. Ultimately, *make an authentic connection—* if you are being yourself and believing in the medicine you have to offer, that will come through.

Make the Assessment Healing

Many healers do assessments when the work commences. If that is something you do, find a way to make the assessment healing. You don't have to just hand someone a form and watch them fill it out or ask someone invasive questions as they answer, with little conversation about the answers. When you ask questions, you can reflect things back that let this person know you see them, or that you are making a small but meaningful connection already. However you help heal people, find a way to do a small version of that during the assessment and introduction period. Not a version that is going to send them to the most painful parts of their trauma or to total despair about their physical health; just something that helps them feel seen, heard, and cared for. That could be as simple as being nonjudgmental and making eye contact; it will differ for each person.

Work in a Space That Demonstrates Your Values

We can't always control the environment where we work, and this is especially true when we first start out. Often, new practitioners are using other people's spaces until they build up their own practices enough to warrant their own office. Some practitioners share an office throughout their career. However, you can make an attempt to create a reasonably pleasant environment to work in. What people put in their offices and the general state of the space say a lot, and clients are often listening on that level even if they never comment openly about it. I once went to someone's office and it was so filthy I didn't want to touch anything. It hadn't been cleaned in years. The white leather chair was so dirty I could have peeled solid chunks of grime off with my fingernails. They were trying to sublet the space to me for a few days per week. I was disturbed by the level of filth and I quickly left. The person showing the office to me clearly has issues with neglecting the space, and that was not something I wanted to communicate to people. If you are a little messy, that is fine, you are a human, but people don't want to do their healing work surrounded by your self-neglect issues. If you wonder how your office appears to others, have a few colleagues check it out, and ask for honest feedback.

If you work from home using a virtual method, remember that the space your clients can see in the background is impactful and that the things they don't see (but you are aware of) are impactful too. If you are working in a room that is messy and used for many other tasks, it may be hard to drop into the work while you also stare at three loads of laundry and an unfinished project from two months ago. Remember that you have needs, and just because the things offscreen aren't visible to the client doesn't mean that they don't impact you. Sometimes people who work virtually and practice in a dual-purpose space (e.g., their bedroom or their kitchen) can struggle with feeling engulfed or that there is not enough separation from their work. It may not appear as clearly as that; it could just emerge as a sense of dread about practicing or procrastination regarding scheduling appointments. Energetically speaking, if you must see your clients in the same space where you sleep, do something to transition the space from office time to home time.

* * *

While many of these suggestions are geared toward practitioners who are just starting out, soliciting feedback about your public-facing materials and your first contact can be useful at any point in your path. It could be in the first month of working or ten years in; if you are having problems building a sustainable practice, this is a great place to bring more attention. When there is an issue, just go right to the edge of your knowledge about it and bring more curiosity. Finally, if you are struggling for a long time to create a full practice, I highly encourage you to go to therapy and start working on whatever relational issues are emerging. Often, your issues can be quite opaque to you but very obvious to someone else. When things really are not working, it typically points to a need for more personal healing. When people come to meet you, they can feel and intuit how much personal work you have done. Being a healing practitioner means that we need to have done a lot of our own personal work. That doesn't mean that you don't get to be a human and have flaws—you can have trillions of those. But you need to have done some deep work on yourself to be able to hold space for others to do the same.

10.1 *Body Scan*

Using the same body scan from chapter 1 (or do a shorter version by focusing on your breath, your heart/chest, and your belly), ask yourself the question: how was this chapter for you? Listen to your body for the answer.

10.2 *Writing*

1. What do you do when you are anxious?

2. What is your existing relationship to people contacting you?

3. When you get texts or emails, are you excited, do you get annoyed, do you find that you were waiting for them, or do you feel easily overwhelmed by contact?

10.3 *Review Your Materials*

If you already have an existing practice, have a trusted colleague call your voicemail, look over your social media presence, use your scheduling software, and visit your website, and then give you honest feedback about how it all lands.

If you do not have a practice yet, reflect on what it has been like for you as a client or a person accessing a service of any kind. What is important to you in that process? How do you want it to make you feel? What kind of information do you need in order to choose to work with someone?

As a higher-risk option (which could result in painful but important feedback)—if you don't have a practice yet, ask a trusted friend about how your communication and the general manner in which you make connection lands with them. Remember that even hard-to-hear feedback is a gift.

===== *REVIEW AND SHIFTING FOCUS* =====

To this point we have covered the basics of the internal work required to hone your intentions, as well as the process of bringing those intentions to the larger world, outside of yourself.

In the following chapters we will explore more about the path of healership by contextualizing the work in some of the larger systems, both current and historical, that we exist within.

Allowing Love

Reflections on Class and Practice-Building

Most books that venture into the realm of self-help business support have at least one chapter on making money. Typically, they will encourage you to make money beyond what you had previously imagined for yourself. Couched in self-help-style language, it is a narrative of you finally being empowered enough to take a seat at the table of the rich. Some of them even include fantasies in the form of experiential exercises that invite you to imagine things like the house you live in, the vacation home, the leisurely mornings when you barely work but still earn ... well, in case you haven't picked up on it yet: that is not where this is going.

While I want to support you to be financially sustained, this book and the principles within it are grounded in not creating more harm. Within capitalist culture we can become confused about the difference between "financially sustained" and a state of amassing and hoarding wealth that perpetuates exploitation and violence. I consider greed to be one of the most normalized and unquestioned substance abuse issues within capitalist culture.

Underlying most addiction issues are emotional and spiritual wounds. If finally achieving a sustainable income was enough to heal those wounds, there would not be a need to keep earning. However, as with the use of any substance to manage emotional and spiritual issues, many people develop a tolerance and need to increase their use. Even people who are not in a full-blown substance abuse relationship with money can overidentify with it as a way to soothe wounds. However, the disappointing reality is that there is not an income level that one will ever reach that can cure emotional or spiritual pain. Only love can do that.

Money promises some opportunities that are quite beneficial, and I would never want to downplay that. Within this critique I am not asserting that you excessively restrict yourself, ignore your needs, or refrain from reasonable saving. However, culturally speaking, we do a substantial amount of fantasizing about what money can do, and we ignore much of the evidence about its limitations. Rich people die young, feel lonely, feel shame, feel afraid, can be heartbroken, and get bored. Because they are humans. *No amount of money or lack thereof will ever let you escape your own humanity.*

I want to support you to be *sustained* as a healing practitioner, and sustaining this path is not only about money. What sustains you will be a very personal combination of elements, and I hope through this book you have been able to develop a deeper curiosity about what that is.

What we *will* do in this chapter is look at some common ways that class experience impacts practice-building and we'll consider the role that love has in addressing those impacts. While this chapter will not include financial education such as budgeting, setting a pay scale, or tracking expenses, that is an area where I highly encourage you to seek support and gain new skills if you do not already have them. Finally, I want to acknowledge that talking about class issues, and especially wealth access, can elicit defensiveness. It can be difficult to confront coping strategies that involve money, as capitalist culture has attached a level of shame to finances that produces an understandable fear. As you read this chapter, try to do so with an open mind. Note any defensiveness and attempt to engage with it consciously.

* * *

When I was in college I mentioned to a classmate that I had grown up in poverty. An awkward look of shock appeared on his face and he quickly proclaimed, "Don't worry, you come off as very smart and I totally couldn't tell." Most people aren't so unaware of themselves to say something that blatantly classist, but I knew he wasn't saying anything that other people didn't think. It wasn't the first or last time someone would exclaim with shock that they would never guess such a thing about me, as though it was a reassuring compliment rather than an assertion that poverty is (1) shameful and (2) linked with lacking intelligence. Experiences like that exchange reified my sense that when I was in predominantly middle- to owning-class spaces (such as college or professional environments), hiding my class experience was the only way to fit in with my peers. However, hiding meant that in those spaces no one really knew me. A friend in high school and a friend in grad school both said almost the identical statement to me fourteen years apart: "I know so much about what you think and what your ideas are, but I don't feel like I know anything about you." Hiding had become second nature.

Growing up in poverty, I spent a lot of time fantasizing that having more money would relieve me of my problems. But more than relieving me of the material problems of my life, I thought that having money would put an end to the unbearable shame of poverty. With money, I imagined, I could hide even better. I felt that somehow the ways I was made to feel utterly worthless, undeserving of affordable health care, housing security, and adequate heat through cold winters—would all disappear with a bigger paycheck.

After I became a licensed therapist and started to earn a higher income, I was elated. I can tell you, truly, money solves a lot of problems. The ease of entering a grocery store and choosing foods without fear of the cost; going to the doctor, because I could afford my co-pay; putting my rent on auto-pay, because I was sure there would be enough in my account by the first of the month—money makes many basic needs far more accessible. Some of my "mental health issues" were reasonable anxieties born out of poverty. That is why I encourage everyone to charge enough to be well.

While my anxiety was lessening, an unfamiliar disappointment set in. Shame is not relieved by money. Money couldn't buy love from others and it certainly couldn't buy self-love, which was in short supply for me. It had been more than a decade since I had last been called "white trash" by a peer, but I walked through life feeling that degraded regardless. Relief from the shame arrived only when I was no longer afraid to be honest about what my life has been like, and to know in the deepest parts of my soul: poverty was never my fault and there is nothing to be ashamed of about being in need. If you live on the street, live in a trailer, or live in a mansion—your inherent goodness as a human being is the same and you deserve respect. In short: I needed to love myself.

Over the years that I've supported healers in practice-building I have observed that class experience greatly impacts this process, for better or worse. In previous personal stories throughout this book I have shared about feeling hyperconscious of my appearance to the point that I didn't enjoy going to work, my issues with chronically undercharging, and my struggles with asserting boundaries related to cancellations. Part of what fueled all this was lack of self-esteem, stemming from class shame. In addition to those issues, I felt like an imposter. I worried about my colleagues and my clients somehow discovering I was a fake. And I overfunctioned within healing relationships, not asking my clients to work hard enough in their own healing. I inappropriately saw their underfunctioning as my responsibility—poverty is the experience of being told by society that the poor are more responsible for the labor that makes the world turn, rather than that labor being a shared effort. Ultimately I felt fairly alone in the larger community of professionals because I was still hiding myself. I was mistrusting of new colleagues. While I had good reason to feel worried, because classism abounds in the field of psychotherapy, there were people who *could* be my allies, or actual fellow peers who shared a similar class experience as mine.

Even if the scene I just described was reasonably sustainable for a short amount of time—I had a job, I had a few colleagues I felt connected to, I had several "professional" sweaters, I was okay—zooming out to the larger picture, this was far from sustainable. I was perpetuating my class wounding by re-constellating it at every turn.

In chapter three, I spoke about how undercharging was negatively impacting my life (struggling to pay student loans, the likelihood I would never save for retirement); however, undercharging doesn't just negatively impact the practitioner. When Elizabeth and my father died, I was a waitress. While no one should have to work while they are grieving, I had a job where I could work and be miserable. As a therapist, I cannot subject my clients to whatever hell my psyche goes through when I am in that much pain. For their sake, I need to charge enough to have a backup plan for times when it is unreasonable to see them. But when I started my practice I did not understand that, as I had never had a job that offered paid time off, paid sick days, health insurance, or any benefits other than a daily shift meal and tips. For me, the situation actually felt very plush in comparison to my previous circumstances. Often, people who live through poverty have a very high tolerance for the pain of unmet needs, which can result in not even noticing that something is wrong or, in my case, that I had the power to change it. I use the word "change" in a very specific manner. I will be living with some of the financial impacts of poverty for the rest of my life and I have had to accept that I cannot change that. There are numerous, painful sacrifices I have made to earn a reasonable income, and it feels important to name this because otherwise it sounds as if I am implying that anyone could change their class experience if they just woke up and accepted responsibility for it. What I *did* realize I was able to change was my relationship to how I structured the finances of my practice so that I could earn a higher income. This realization was an act of love.

While not everyone reading this is going to relate to the particulars of my class experience, in helping healers build a practice I have observed that regardless of class background, we are a field of people who really struggle to value our work, especially for early-career practitioners. How did I end up building a far more sustainable practice? One of the things that was really holding me back was my refusal to accept how dependent I am on other people. This is a huge class issue and it plays out differently for different class experiences. From my observations many people who can afford to will opt to avoid mutual interdependence through money, by paying people for services and avoiding asking for help from more intimate relationships. Whereas people with less financial access tend to give and receive mutual support within community, or be self-reliant and straight-up ignore their personal needs. In charging enough, I had to face the brutal and uncomfortable truth of how deeply dependent I am on my clients. I need them to survive. And they also need me to survive. But I was engaging with them as though I could survive on barely anything while giving them a lot, which is frankly impossible. While bursting the bubble of my fear of dependency might sound easy, it was excruciating. I had to face the incredible pain of needing so much as a child but being so deprived. However, if I did not do that work I would end up resenting my clients. And resentment in healing relationships is toxic to both people.

In acknowledging my dependency, I had to become clear on my boundaries regarding fees and a sliding scale. I promised to myself that for the sake of my clients and my own well-being that I would stick very strictly to those boundaries, even if it was extremely uncomfortable.

As I describe the ways that I concretely changed my practice, I want to highlight that all of this was possible only because my heart grew. Where previously I could love only the parts of myself that were competent and self-reliant, my heart expanded to include the parts of me that were needy, ashamed, afraid, and hurt. It was through love that I found my way.

Class is extremely complex and it impacts each of us in very different and sometimes very similar ways. In addition to my personal account of class shame related to poverty, I want to point out that many people who have wealth privilege feel ashamed and confused about the ways it has wounded them. It can be hard to name the wounding when the dominant narrative of wealth is that being rich somehow prevents pain. *Don't the rich have perfect lives?* No, people of all class backgrounds can experience abuse, wounding, and the general suffering of being alive. People experiencing poverty are suffering a very severe form of societal abuse that the middle to owning class are not. And classism is intimately and uniquely shaped by racism, as well as ableism, sexism, transphobia, and other oppressions. My assertion that we all experience wounding is in no way an attempt to equate these woundings, nor is it an attempt to erase the combined abuse of classism and any other form of oppression. Rather, I am making the point that the toxicity of exploitation spares no one, not even the people who benefit from it. Furthermore, no one has a *comfortable* relationship with money. Some people may seem that way; often, people who *have* money seem comfortable with it. But capitalism is tremendously harmful. Achieving a comfortable relationship to something harmful is more of an ongoing, dynamic process than something one achieves and sustains forever. Additionally, without close examination, denial, complacency, and dissociation can oddly appear like comfort.

All this said, the big exercise I encourage you to do in response to reading this chapter is to write a comprehensive history about your class experience, explore how it is impacting your current practice or the way that you are thinking about building a practice, and consider where love is needed in all its forms to assist you in healing (you will find more on this in the exercises at the end of the chapter).

Let's turn now to talking about some of the common ways class issues impact practice-building. Remember that class is complicated, and although I am giving examples, your actual experience may vary. I am intentionally not defining class experiences such as "middle class," "mixed class," and other class labels, because I find those to be flattening of people's real experiences. While those labels are useful in talking about broad groups of people, I want to support you to explore class through a very personal lens that allows you to consider the ways all parts of your identity intersect with your class experience. Throughout this chapter I do use terms referencing class groups, because language is limited and makes it unavoidable. In some circumstances, the following issues and scenarios I will describe can stem from trauma that is not directly related to class; however, I won't be focusing on that here, in order to make some important points about class issues.

Lack of Ability to Envision a Path

Knowing what you want to do with your life, who you want to work with, and other specifics of your path is a skill. While it is a skill that many suffer from not having, it tends to be something middle- to owning-class people struggle with often. My wealthier peers have frequently expressed that they envy my ability to take action, know who I am, and what I want to do. At first this produced a state of confusion within me; however, over time their envy has helped me understand that growing up with very little forced me to take action, work hard, and identify myself in the world. Growing up with excess disconnects people from their sense of hunger. It is hard to know what you want when a meal is eternally placed in front of you. Additionally, many owning-class people are force-fed their "purpose," the purpose that their family and society deems worthy of their "status." Being forced to live one's life based on the preferences of someone else, as a means to demonstrate status, is a form of wounding and neglect. It can substantially distort any existing relationship to personal truth. For healers with this wounding, it can be hard to choose a path that people they love and admire may be critical about. The alternative option is to live a life with less meaning and be controlled by the desires of others. It isn't easy and includes some pain to live one's passions when that includes loss of respect or love from family. But it also isn't loving to yourself to deny your purpose.

Feeling Unworthy of a Practice or a Path

People of all class experiences can struggle with feeling unworthy of having a path. This may manifest as knowing what you want or need, but denying it. In practice-building that could mean playing small, avoiding taking action, or generally struggling to build a clientele out of lack of self-esteem. Many poor and working-class people do not feel allowed to have a path due to being shamed into feeling inferior. However, as I touched on in a previous chapter, people with ample privilege can feel guilty about having a path, because others do not have that choice. While it may be true that you will be allowed to live out a chosen path in ways that others will not, ignoring your path does not liberate anyone. In both these circumstances there is a need for more love for yourself and your potential clients (who need your help).

Undercharging

As I demonstrated in my personal narrative, poverty greatly impacts the ability to charge enough, as a result of shame and not valuing one's offerings. However, people with financial privilege struggle with this too. In that context it seems to be more of a combination of guilt and shame about charging for offerings while the practitioner may not be experiencing much actual financial need. For people with a small amount of wealth privilege, undercharging can be a serious financial concern over time, as they may not be earning enough and may be accruing debt. For people with substantial privilege, undercharging won't really matter in a material way, but it will matter in an emotional way. Keeping your rates low out of guilt and shame produces resentment, regardless of the level of need the practitioner has. Even if after doing a lot of personal work around the shame and guilt, the practitioner decides not to raise their rates, it still makes a difference because the rates now feel like a consensual choice for the practitioner, rather than a form of soothing or compulsion related to unresolved feelings of guilt.

In more politically left healing communities, undercharging can be construed as a pious or virtuous trait, rather than a result of unhealed wounds. One reason this perspective is popular is that while being a "good person" in a capitalist context means earning excessively, in a politically left environment achieving the status of being "good" can be dependent on the level to which one is rejecting earning or appears to be struggling. Embedded in this perspective is the desire to be accepted by peers and to find esteem through deprivation and fabricated moral superiority. When poor people engage in this dynamic, it re-creates the trauma of poverty. Underlying this value system is the sense that "I will be good once I don't need anything." It is an understandable way to cope with being shamed for having needs, but it doesn't result in a sustainable healing practice. When this perspective is espoused by people with wealth privilege (and often white privilege), it re-creates existing oppressive systems. Requiring that healers be willing to work below a living wage in order to be politically acceptable by the left creates an expectation that can be filled only by people with access to previously amassed wealth. It is a subtly classist and racist ideology. Promoting reasonable compensation for healing practitioners supports poor and working-class people to enter the field, which in turn supports people of color who are disproportionately forced into poverty by racism. Additionally, depriving one's self of financial income as a means to avert wealth-based shame is ineffective and robs the practitioner of the opportunity to grow a healthy sense of self-acceptance and self-love.

Discussing Fees and Maintaining a Sustainable Sliding Scale

Discussing money is often uncomfortable for healers and the people we work with. It is important that you grow skills to talk about money, even if it is uncomfortable. However, just because you do the work doesn't mean it will be an easeful conversation. Talking about money specifically related to accessing care can elicit shame, fear, guilt, anger, and grief from clients. At times those feelings can be directed at us, as though we are responsible for the creation of them. It can be hard to be loving when a client is acting out about something that links so closely to your needs. Still, cultivating a loving conversation around money that centers integrity is essential. Remember that being loving doesn't equate to having no boundaries or needs.

Some healers try to avoid talking about money by never raising their fees and not having a sliding scale. While that can work for awhile, the cost of living increases, and you may eventually make your practice unstable by undercharging. And I would like to encourage you to have a sliding scale, if you can afford to, as it helps to make healing accessible.

Discussing fees is an arena where the class experience of the healer and that of the client are in direct communication. Whatever your cultural norms are related to discussing money may be a good match with a client or may cause conflict. Before I did substantial healing work regarding money, I would occasionally end up feeling shamed by wealthier clients, as though discussing money is "low class." On the other hand, at times it has felt reparative, with wealthier clients expressing a longing to compensate me fairly. With lower-income clients the conversation at times feels more culturally familiar and easeful for me, but at other times it has felt charged with fear (for both of us).

Some people have sliding scales wherein the client self-appoints based on their own assessment or an assessment you provide (i.e., the client chooses their fee on their own, without conversation, based on the scale you present or based on income brackets that correspond to certain fees). As a provider who sees people weekly, I have little room for my sliding scale to be inaccurate. If I was a healer who saw someone only once, I might be more flexible and have a self-appointed scale. However, if I have seven clients who have self-appointed below what they can actually pay, that limits spaces for people who actually need them, and I would be committed to that income on a weekly basis. For this reason my sliding scale involves a conversation about the client's financial situation. At times a potential client has called and asked for a reduced fee, and when prompted to say more about why and what their needs are, they respond in offended shock that I would ask such a personal question. When someone acts shocked that you would discuss money, it can feel shaming—especially for lower-income clinicians. In my experience that response mostly comes from owning/upper-class people whose cultural conditioning holds the narrative that discussing money is off-limits and who may not have a concrete relationship to the mutuality of the financial exchange. Poor people have had their finances scrutinized by government assistance programs ad nauseam. Most people who have experienced poverty do not balk at the question and, unfortunately, actually expect it. This type of scrutiny places poor people in the role of having to prove their poverty, which is oppressive. The result is that poor people tend to speak more freely about their class experiences than people from the middle or owning class. That doesn't mean they will be free of fear or that the interaction won't be awkward, as asking for a reduced fee can be vulnerable and fear-inducing. Though I do not want to ask anyone to prove their level of need, in my experience it is a necessary conversation, because at times wealthy people try to access low-fee services without having a real need for the reduced fee. Wealth produces entitlement, which can result in feeling much more comfortable asking someone else to financially sacrifice for one's comforts. However, there is always room to make the conversation more loving and equitable. Discussing money doesn't need to re-create the harms of capitalism for you or the people you serve.

Being Overly Picky or Prideful

I fully support you to be choosy and work with people who are good fits. However, there is a difference between being discerning based on finding the right fit, and being overly picky to protect one's pride. Being early in your practice is vulnerable and shame-inducing. Here are some things I have heard new clinicians say about rejecting potential clients: "I don't want to work for so little; I am worth more than that" or "I envisioned myself working with people who are more interesting/alternative/professional/artistic [than whoever the practitioner just turned down]" or "I only want to work a few hours per week, because I want a lot of leisure time, so I turned down the client" or "That person just seemed too unwell for me to work with them; they seemed annoying." The list could go on and on.

Why do some practitioners behave in such a picky manner, and how does it relate to class issues? Some of this is more apparent: not wanting to work for a lower fee (when it is not a financial burden to do so) can be a result of attaching your sense of self-esteem to money. And some of it is less apparent: out of necessity, poor and working-class people tend to be more accepting of clients who come to them, whereas wealthier people can fall into the trap of being overly controlling of their lives and who is included in that life. Wealth privilege allows a lot of control over who one has to interact with. One might be able to pick and choose who is around them, never depending on anyone in uncomfortable ways; but amid that control is a loss of contact with spontaneity, wonder, mystery, and chance. Overcontrolling one's own life produces a lack of opportunity to learn to tolerate things that are uncomfortable, and contributes to the destruction of aliveness. All of these options are unfortunate for healing practitioners because we need to be in contact with our aliveness in order to sustain our work. Being able to be picky is easier for people with the wealth access to sustain themselves without clients, but what may feel like a privilege generally results in a brutal sense of shame. It doesn't matter how much money you have; engaging with your true purpose is what allows for a robust and loving sense of pride. Many people are overly picky because they actually feel insecure. Poor people are just forced to cope with this rapidly, whereas rich people can avoid it for longer. Some poor people do engage in being overly picky and it is extremely stressful, which is a form of reenacting class-based trauma. It takes a lot of self-love to endure the insecurities that come with having a fledgling practice. If being overly picky describes you at all, cultivating love is the first step toward breaking this pattern.

Lacking Discernment

A close cousin to being overly picky is the opposite problem of not being discerning enough. There are people you should not work with for many reasons, a few examples being: lack of competency, lack of functional rapport, or they trigger your unhealed trauma. People who are worried about money tend to make too many exceptions, because it can be very hard to turn away income. While it is good to be open and to try working with many types of people, lack of discernment can lead to burnout. Working with someone just because they can pay you, when it is not actually a good fit, can be very draining. This dynamic is also not good for the client, who needs a practitioner who feels engaged and well in the relationship. While the solution to this pattern is complicated—the clinician does need stable income—love is still a part of the answer. You have to love your well-being enough to protect it. And you have to love others enough to say "no" when it is not a good fit.

Lacking Financial Literacy

Financial literacy is very important in running a practice. While I love to talk about spirituality till the cows come home, if you don't have the material reality of your books in order, your practice will suffer. Many people report feeling embarrassed about lacking this type of literacy. From that place it can be compelling to ignore it or not ask for help, but it is actually critical for the sustainability of your life that you work up the self-love and courage to get support. Poverty can produce a lack of literacy, because there is simply not much that needs to be managed. If no one in your family has ever run a business, the finances could be as simple as cashing a paycheck and paying the bills as often as is possible. Wealthier people often develop some literacy, but a common issue in wealthy families is controlling dynamics around money. So, some wealthy people end up knowing very little about their finances due to controlling superior family members. As well, some people don't know much about finances because they have paid someone else to manage that part of their lives. Whatever the reason may be, if you do not understand how to build adequate systems for financial management, you will need to learn about this.

Overworking, Workaholism, and Burnout

Burnout for healer professions is a huge issue! It takes so much to sustain this work and there are many people in need—it can be hard to say "no." However, burning out results in not enjoying your path as a healer, as well as giving less than optimal services.

In the land of capitalism, it is easy to feel that productivity is what makes you a good person. This is especially true for people raised in class environments that demanded they work very hard. Poor and working-class people are encouraged to work beyond the physical comfort of their bodies, and this can easily be constellated in a healing practice. While society may treat you as though your body and psyche do not matter, they do. Offering excellent healing services requires that you prioritize the well-being of your body and lovingly accept your true limits, rather than the ones society has tried to force upon you.

While workaholism could seem like it is only about making money, which it could be for some, more often it is about aggrandizing the self through accomplishments, important commitments, being needed, and generally appearing hypercompetent. In a sense it is a defense against shame. The antidote to shame is love and acceptance. While workaholism can be something that manifests unrelated to class, many people learn this coping strategy from having work-addicted parents.

A final comment on workaholism: it can be difficult to detect because capitalist culture celebrates overworking and there can be positive feedback and regard from peers. Be curious with yourself about what the signs are that you need a break. It may take years to come to that awareness, but eventually finding where your limits lie is integral to a sustainable practice.

* * *

The examples I presented are not an exhaustive list, as that would be impossible. However, I hope they can serve as a jumping-off point for you to think critically about how your own class experience impacts your path of healership.

On Offering Gifts

While I strongly encourage you to charge enough to sustain yourself, I caution you against seeing your time as always related to money. Or finding yourself unwilling to do things that are unpaid. Giving gifts or volunteering produces gratitude and community. It is also an esteemable act that can actually help to repair a sense of esteem that has been wounded. As I described in an earlier chapter, in 2019 I made a podcast that I spent more than five hundred hours of unpaid time working on. It was a gift. It was an iteration of my life's work to help people understand the spiritual wounds of sexual violence and methods of healing those wounds. I gave it freely because I want everyone to have that information, should they seek it. I gave it freely because it is something I *could* give. I cannot give my time endlessly without compensation, but I can give my labor in the form of a document that people can access forever. I have felt an outpouring of community support because of that gift, as well as a sense of pride. Gifts are given without expectation of something in return; however, there is often reciprocity. My life has been enriched in ways I could not have imagined. I feel moved to tears when people share with me how much it has impacted them. Giving is "awe"-some. And it is a tiny way you can push back against capitalism, to keep the gift alive.

On Allowing Love

Capitalism is alienating and produces varying types of isolation depending on your class experience. With any of the financial-emotional dynamics outlined in this chapter, remember that you do not need to heal alone. This is a collective effort. The class-related issues that people suffer from are real and important concerns that *everyone* deserves space to transform. With every scenario I described, in some abstract way *love is always the answer.* Whether that is increased love for yourself or for others, love offers us the compassion and respect required to live in the highest integrity possible. When we have to say "no" to someone, when we have to make a business budget for the first time, and when we must humbly ask for help—we can do it all with love. That is, of course, only possible if you are able to allow love. We are born as loving creatures. Babies soak up and emit love. It is through the wounds we incur in life that we lose the capacity to love ourselves, other people, Earth, and all its inhabitants.

Allowing love is the antithesis to amassing wealth. Allowing love is about valuing the quality of your relationships. It is about the unparalleled intimacy of depending on others and being there for them in return. It is about loving yourself and all life enough to do the laborious work of parsing out what you need financially from what you do not. It is about accepting your limits as a human being. It is about knowing that you will not always be happy or well, but you will hopefully be in community with people who love you back. It is about understanding what tool does what job; money will not solve emotional and spiritual problems—love does that.

* * *

Before Elizabeth Bolles passed away, she told me I had to work out my "class issues." At the time I felt embarrassed to hear the words come out of her mouth. I was so defended against my pain that I wanted to ignore their meaning. However, despite my attempt to forget what she had said, her voice followed me. It took years to really understand what she was pointing me toward. I am eternally grateful for that and for much of the other wisdom she offered. I will offer you the same advice: work out your class issues. Work them out, because *class issues are love issues.*

11.1 *Body Scan*

Using the same body scan from chapter 1 (or do a shorter version by focusing on your breath, your heart/chest, and your belly), ask yourself the question: what did this chapter bring up for you? Listen to your body for the answer.

11.2 *Sharing and Witnessing*

For a variety of reasons people from different class backgrounds struggle to discuss money. This exercise is an opportunity to challenge yourself around growing skills to talk about money and class with others. Find a trusted friend or colleague you can explore the topic of money and class with, and try having a conversation with these questions:

1. Where did you learn about money?

2. What does money represent to you?

3. Have you ever tried to soothe with money or with the rejection of it, and if so what are some specific examples?

4. What are the underlying emotional issues that come up around your class experience?

5. What ways do you think your class experience may impact building a practice?

6. Is there a need for more self-love and/or love of others in how you engage with money, class, and your healing practice?

11.3 *Ritual Conversation*

Once you get clear on some of what emotional material has come up for you regarding class, set the table for tea and have a conversation with this material. You could actually set up a ritual tea space or just imagine this space in your mind. Either way, make it intentional space and give yourself the time to see where the conversation takes you. If you don't know where to start, ask this underlying emotional material to tell you more about its hopes, its fears, and what it might need to feel loved. Anytime that you are hosting a guest, you thank the guest for coming and you make sure that the guest is comfortable—host this guest as you would host any important guest.

11.4 *Writing*

In this exercise I encourage you to write a comprehensive history about your class experience, explore how it is impacting your current practice or the way that you are thinking about building a practice, and consider where love is needed in all its forms to assist you in healing. Class is extremely complicated, encompassing culture, financial access, type of career, how much one's body is used in work, generational experience versus current experience, and so much more. And many people have a mixed class experience, which can result in a variety of coping strategies and narratives around money. It can be helpful to go back as many generations as you have knowledge of to learn about the class experiences of your parents, grandparents, and even great-grandparents. Class is also intimately related to many other parts of identity; let your narrative reflect all parts of you. Here are some simple prompts to help you get started:

1. What do you know about your class experience?

2. What was the class experience of the person or people who raised you?

3. What brings you pride about your class experience?

4. What is hard to face about your class experience?

5. How can you see your class experience influencing your thinking or actions around your practice? If you do not have a practice yet, how is class impacting your ability to be on your path?

6. What parts of your experience have been wounding and need healing?

7. What parts of your experience need more love and acceptance?

Degradation of Healership
and the Path Forward

Throughout this book I have pointed to the issue of low self-esteem being rampant among healers. We have explored various reasons why it can be hard to value our work—trauma, wounding, and being the target of societal abuse. However, I want to turn toward looking at larger systems of oppression from a historical viewpoint in order to illustrate a centuries-long devaluing of the lineage of healership itself. From there I will touch on the depoliticizing of healing and the path forward.

The transition from feudalism to capitalism, as Silvia Federici details in her book *Caliban and the Witch*, was facilitated by the European witch trials and predicated on the devaluing of and making invisible the reproductive labor of women. She states, "[women's] work was defined as a natural resource, laying outside the sphere of market relations."[8] Healership is often associated with women, and I would argue some of that association is born from the emotional aspects of reproductive labor: the work of tending to humanity through parenting and providing general care at family and community levels. The degradation of feminized labor is simultaneously the degradation of the work of healers.

The witch trials of Europe spanned roughly three hundred years, from 1450 to 1750. The bulk of the trials occurred over a hundred-year period, from the mid-1500s to the mid-1600s. During the peak of the trials the newly forming European states worked in tandem with the Christian church to torture and murder tens of thousands[9] of women; a form of class war, most of the victims were poor. This capitalistic misogyny impacts more than just European women, as it has been forcibly exported around the world, including witch trials of the same period in the Americas. In Europe and the Americas, the witch-hunts made a specific target out of magic and Indigenous spirituality. Federici states, "Though the witch-hunt targeted a broad variety of female practices, it was above all in this capacity—as sorcerers, healers, performers of incantations and divinations—that women were persecuted."[10] The witch trials were a three-hundred-year-long misogynist attack on healership and poverty with reverberations extending to today.

Intimately connected to the devaluing of feminized labor, the transition to capitalism, and the degradation of healership is forced Christianization. History provides several examples of forced Christianization: the Crusades, the Inquisition, the European-perpetrated witch trials, American chattel slavery, colonization by the Holy Roman Empire, and European colonization. Forced Christianization is the process by which the Christian church vilified, punished, tortured, and murdered Muslims, Jews, people practicing earth-based spiritualities, Africans, Indigenous people, and heretics in order to either convert or exterminate alternative spiritual views. For centuries the Christian church has participated in unspeakable violence, taking the lives of countless individuals in the name of power and control. This too is a degradation of healership: spirituality is foundational to healing, as are intact culture, elders, generational knowledge, and access to a traditional land base. Forcing people to become Christian, policing their thoughts, and murdering their elders or spiritual leaders creates a crisis in the healing capacity of the surviving community. While the church destroyed people's access to healing knowledge, the European capitalist elites destroyed access to traditional lands on their own soil and abroad. The forced relocation inherent in American chattel slavery and the privatizing of land through theft, displacement, and genocide are all methods Europeans used to disconnect people from their traditional land base.

Capitalism and forced Christianization are also intertwined with the project of colonization, which centers around domination, dehumanization, and spiritual degradation of Indigenous populations. Colonization has resulted in the devastating and continuing loss of Indigenous people's healing practices. Inherent in colonial American society and its continued legacy is the degradation of Indigenous and African life and labor, and ultimately the lives and labor of people of color in general. Federici states, "While the response to the population crisis [not enough labor] in Europe was the subjugation of women to reproduction, in colonial America, where colonization destroyed ninety five percent of the aboriginal population, the response was the slave trade which delivered to the European ruling class an immense quantity of labor-power."[11] In the contemporary field of healing, this capitalistic racism manifests in a myriad of ways, including the wage discrepancy between practitioners of color and white practitioners, and a specific devaluing and undercompensating related to the healing practices of Indigenous or African origins.

In a capitalist and colonialist landscape that disregards thousands of years of ancestral wisdom, wherein many knowledge bases have been completely destroyed, there can be a lot of confusion about how healing works, for both the healer and the person seeking healing. Suffering from doubt that healing is possible is a normal response to being socialized in environments that degrade it. That degradation can result in healers struggling with self-esteem and, at times, the client struggling to value the healing relationship.

Why does capitalism require healers and healing to be degraded? Why has the Christian church systematically attempted to destroy most other spiritual traditions? Speaking about the church's anti-heretic endeavors, Federici points out:

> Heresy was the equivalent of "liberation theology" for the medieval proletariat. It gave a frame to peoples' demands for spiritual renewal and social justice, challenging both the Church and secular authority by appeal to a higher truth. It denounced social hierarchies, private property and the accumulation of wealth, and it disseminated among the people a new, revolutionary aspect of daily life (work, property, sexual reproduction, and the position of women), posing the question of emancipation in truly universal terms.[12]

Spirituality has been a primary location of social control and violence within the Western tradition of domination because it carries the promise of liberation. Violence is an interruption in connection to spirit, for both the perpetrator and the victim. To varying degrees, we are all wounded by these larger systems of oppression. Spiritual liberation is dangerous, a form of self-defense, because it represents the power to heal, which allows us to resist, to take accountability for harm and invest ourselves in the well-being of all life, or both.

While many people have embraced Christianity and experience it as a source of liberation (which I in no way intend to shame or degrade), understanding the historical intention behind *forced* Christianization is important. There is a conflict of interest between healers and the governing powers of church and state, as those systems of power do not thrive on the embodied, liberated, and spiritually well state of their subjects. Those systems have a vested interest in sustaining the conditions that make humanity unwell.

While contemporary mainstream culture may appear to embrace healing, efforts to strip the inherent liberatory and political nature of it abound. Ruling powers both governmental and capitalistic have started to use methods emerging from thousands of years of tradition with significant alterations. Healing that comes from entheogenic plants such as Iboga, Peyote, Ayahuasca, San Pedro, and psilocybin-containing mushrooms, as well as Buddhist meditation, call on the recipient, user, or practitioner to engage in long and depthful processes, with emphases on love and stewardship of Earth. In 2020, the US military invested $27 million into developing psychedelics that are rapid acting on issues such as depression, but without the "side effects" of traditional entheogens, such as hallucinations.[13] In the corporate sector, micro-dosing mushrooms is a popular method of increasing productivity among software engineers.[14] The US military is now using time-limited mindfulness sessions to increase soldiers' focus, keeping the meditation under fifteen minutes.[15] These examples have one thing in common: each of them takes a powerful, liberatory ancient healing practice and shortens it or lessens it to make the effect focus on productivity as a worker rather than spiritual health and liberation.

I wasn't always devoted to spirituality. Raised as an atheist, when people in my life referenced God or would say that "love is the answer," I thought they were ridiculous. Ridiculous is a way of saying something is worthy of ridicule. However, as an adult I began to admire healing practitioners who had a spiritual path. I knew that they were connected to *something*—some mysterious source of love and compassion and wisdom. After embracing a spiritual life to the point that I didn't need to make fun of it outside of myself, I began to understand how much I and especially the other white people of colonizer-settler lineage in my life were insecure about being spiritual. We were afraid to talk about love, an essential element of spirituality, in an embodied way. We were afraid to be humiliated by other white people. But we were also just hiding and acting as further agents of colonization and white supremacy. I cannot be an advocate for justice and freedom for all people while I simultaneously reject the spirituality of others as inferior. Many white people of colonizer-settler lineage are attached to degrading spirituality, an ironic sequel to forced Christianization.

While I am highlighting the degradation of healership, I simultaneously want to express that this history impacts each of us beyond our roles as healing practitioners and is not solely one of victimhood (as evidenced by my story above). Some of us are of lineages that have been and continue to be targets of colonization and enslavement. Some of us are a part of a long, horrifically violent effort to enslave, degrade, and destroy the cultures of others, as ours was once degraded and destroyed. Many of us live at the intersection of these forces, carrying the complex lineage of colonized and colonizers.

I want to make a case for the critical importance of healing the impacts of colonialism, slavery, capitalism, and spiritual oppression in each of us. Our clients may come to us seeking healing for something as seemingly unpolitical as intimacy issues or the management of diabetes, yet these ailments are intimately connected to larger systems of oppression. To disregard that connection is a disservice to their health and the health of the world.

Many of our healer-ancestors were murdered for doing this work. And activists, whom I consider to be systemic and community healers, are persecuted and murdered around the globe to this day. Regardless of how much effort is extended by companies and individuals attempting to brand healing as apolitical, and regardless of how many consumers want to adhere to that notion: *healing is political and it is an act of resistance.* In my opinion, the end goal of healing is not to make us better able to function within a capitalist system; it is to liberate us from that system. Let this history remind us of how powerful healers actually are. Your work is extremely important.

The journey of healing can be excruciating. It doesn't matter how you are getting there: it could be through the body, through the mind, or through the spirit. Whether your work is to support people to live or to die (such as death doulas and hospice workers do), whether it is medical, spiritual, or psychological—being a healer will also require you to heal. For some that is easier and for others it can be very painful. For people who are of colonizer-settler lineage, who live in a state of privilege dependent on the degradation of others, facing the guilt and shame is so uncomfortable that many people refuse to heal. For people who are survivors of severe trauma and/or survivors of the worst abuses capitalism and colonialism have inflicted, healing is so difficult that many struggle to do it. And many of us do not fit so neatly into either box, carrying complex and unbearable pain. I cannot overstate how challenging healing can be. Most of us know people who did not survive— those who died slowly through the overuse of substances, those who have taken their own lives, and those who have lost their lives to state, familial, or community violence. The pull to be numb, to turn away, to ease the pain— it is understandable. Becoming a healing practitioner is a commitment to being awake, to turn toward, to live through the pain, so that we may have the strength and the vision to witness and love others as they travel their own path of healing. If being a healer is the work you have been called to do: *do it by healing yourself.* Do it for your ancestors who gave you life; do it for all those who could not heal; do it for future generations of blood and nonblood kin; do it for Earth. All of us—humans, animals, plants, fungi, nonincarnate spirits—are connected in a great web. Your individual healing ripples out and pulls the strings of this great web, connecting you to every other living and nonincarnate being in the collective effort toward liberation.

Low self-esteem and low cultural esteem (the culture of healing) is a part of our collective healership story. All the ways that you may question if you can do it are in part because of a centuries-long history of being told that you cannot. As I've shared previously, in my process of stepping into my path I was plagued with doubts and self-degrading thoughts. It took me ten years to believe I could do it. Through the trials of my own healing, I have learned that self-doubt and low self-esteem are clear results of oppression and that the only way forward in embarking on or sustaining this path is to heal. It might mean that you need to grieve. It might mean that you need to leave an abusive relationship. It might mean that you need to make amends and be accountable for harm. It might mean that you need to break an addiction. It might even mean that you will struggle with an addiction as you become a healer and as you practice. You do not need to be totally healed to do this work. What you need to be is a human, with a heart and a commitment to growth.

Within that great web of all life is a smaller web of healing practitioners. Know that we are beside you. This is the work of your ancestors. It is the work of generations. It existed before capitalism and it will exist after. And beyond the community of human practitioners who may provide holding is the earth and infinite divine love. The inner work required to walk this path is not easy. I realize that I am suggesting you dive deep and process the most painful things you and your lineage have ever endured or perpetrated. Yet, I am still saying no matter what you have to do to heal, give yourself and the world that gift. Love is with you.

12.1 *Body Scan*

Using the same body scan from chapter 1 (or do a shorter version by focusing on your breath, your heart/chest, and your belly), ask yourself the question: what did this chapter bring up for you? What further questions or wonderings do you have? Listen to your body for the answer.

12.2 *Reflection*

1. What is the next step in your path to engage with this history and how it impacts you, and subsequently your healing practice and those around you?

2. What do you want to learn more about and how might you go about finding that information?

3. Are there family members or elders who can help you learn more about your family history and lineage?

12.3 *Writing*

1. What do you know about your ancestors' relationship to spirituality, colonialism, and capitalism?

2. How has this history and the current landscape impacted your healing practice? Or if you do not have a practice yet, how is it impacting your thinking and feeling about starting one?

3. What type of support will you need to *honor* the more personal ways this history and the current landscape impact you?

4. What type of support will you need to *heal* the ways this history and the current landscape impact you?

5. What is the history of your healing modality? Where did it come from and how has it been treated in relationship to capitalism, spiritual oppression, and colonialism?

A Prayer

I call on spirit to grant you some form of relationship in this lifetime that will help you heal and guide you in your path.

Whether that is a very attuned therapist, a guiding elder, amazing colleagues, a supportive partner(s), a ride-or-die best friend, or an inspiring community
—whatever it is, may you have the backing of love.

May you honor yourself by stepping fully into your path.
May you feel connected, not just to your ancestors of blood, but your ancestors of craft.
May you take your place in the collective effort of liberation.
May you remember why you do this work.

I call on spirit to support you.
I call on spirit to support you.
I call on spirit to support you.

Notes

1 Audre Lorde, *Sister Outsider: Essays and Speeches* (Trumansburg, NY: Crossing Press, 1984), 53–59.
2 Wilhelm Reich, *The Mass Psychology of Fascism* (New York: Orgone Institute Press, 1946), 25. Translated from the German manuscript.
3 Simon Sinek, "How Great Leaders Inspire Action," TEDxPugetSound, Newcastle, WA, Video, 17:49, September 16, 2009, www.ted.com/talks/simon _sinek_how_great_leaders_inspire_action.
4 William Ronald Dodds Fairbairn, *Psychoanalytic Studies of the Personality* (London: Routledge & Kegan Paul, 1952), 66–67.
5 Heather Kugelmass, "Sorry, I'm Not Accepting New Patients: An Audit Study of Access to Mental Health Care," *Journal of Health and Social Behavior* 57, no. 2 (2016): 168–183.
6 Pat Ogden, Kekuni Minton, and Clare Pain, *Trauma and the Body: A Sensorimotor Approach to Psychotherapy* (New York: W. W. Norton, 2006).
7 The Cosmic Pizza Order comes from many knowledge streams and sources that Eugenia has encountered throughout her path.
8 Silvia Federici, *Caliban and the Witch: Women, the Body and Primitive Accumulation* (New York: Autonomedia, 2014), 97.
9 The exact number of murders is unknown despite the hard work of historians. Estimates range substantially; however, 60,000 to 70,000 deaths is a common estimate.
10 Federici, *Caliban and the Witch*, 174.
11 Federici, *Caliban and the Witch*, 113.
12 Federici, *Caliban and the Witch*, 33.
13 "Roth Leads $26.9 Million Project to Create Better Psychiatric Medications," Newsroom, UNC Health and UNC School of Medicine, June 15, 2020, https:// news.unchealthcare.org/2020/06/roth-leads-26-9-million-project-to-create -better-psychiatric-medications/.

14 Jack Kelly, "Silicon Valley Is Micro-Dosing 'Magic Mushrooms' to Boost Their Careers," *Forbes,* January 17, 2020, www.forbes.com/sites/jackkelly /2020/01/17/silicon-valley-is-micro-dosing-magic-mushrooms-to-boost -their-careers.
15 Matt Richtel, "The Latest in Military Strategy: Mindfulness," *New York Times,* April 5, 2019, www.nytimes.com/2019/04/05/health/military-mindfulness -training.html.

Bibliography

Fairbairn, William Ronald Dodds. *Psychoanalytic Studies of the Personality*. London: Routledge & Kegan Paul, 1952.

Federici, Silvia. *Caliban and the Witch: Women, the Body and Primitive Accumulation*. New York: Autonomedia, 2014.

Kelly, Jack. "Silicon Valley Is Micro-Dosing 'Magic Mushrooms' to Boost Their Careers." *Forbes*, January 17, 2020. www.forbes.com/sites/jackkelly /2020/01/17/silicon-valley-is-micro-dosing-magic-mushrooms-to-boost -their-careers.

Kugelmass, Heather. "Sorry, I'm Not Accepting New Patients: An Audit Study of Access to Mental Health Care." *Journal of Health and Social Behavior* 57, no. 2 (2016): 168–183.

Lorde, Audre. *Sister Outsider: Essays and Speeches*. Trumansburg, NY: Crossing Press, 1984.

Ogden, Pat, Kekuni Minton, and Clare Pain. *Trauma and the Body: A Sensorimotor Approach to Psychotherapy*. New York: W. W. Norton, 2006.

Reich, Wilhelm. *The Mass Psychology of Fascism*. New York: Orgone Institute Press, 1946. Translated from the German manuscript.

Richtel, Matt. "The Latest in Military Strategy: Mindfulness." *New York Times*, April 5, 2019. www.nytimes.com/2019/04/05/health/military-mindfulness -training.html.

"Roth Leads $26.9 Million Project to Create Better Psychiatric Medications." Newsroom, UNC Health and UNC School of Medicine, June 15, 2020. https://news.unchealthcare.org/2020/06/roth-leads-26-9-million-project-to -create-better-psychiatric-medications/.

Sinek, Simon. "How Great Leaders Inspire Action." TEDxPugetSound, Newcastle, WA. Video, 17:49, September 16, 2009. www.ted.com/talks/simon_sinek _how_great_leaders_inspire_action.

Acknowledgments

F irst and foremost, thank you to the plants and molecules that guided me in writing this book and doing the healing necessary to produce it. In no particular order: thank you Ketamine, Noya Rao, Ayahuasca, San Pedro, and 5-MeO-DMT, and much love to the magical mushrooms of Earth.

Thank you Keith Donnell and the North Atlantic Books team for believing in me and offering me the opportunity to write this book.

Thank you Asher for walking through life with me and loving me. I could not have written this book without you.

My dearest Sophie, I could not have completed this book without your love, and I thank you for giving it so generously.

To the many colleagues, friends, and mentors who read the early versions of this book and gave me invaluable, compassionate, and truthful feedback—I offer deep bows of gratitude. Special thanks to Eugenia Guidi, Steuart Gold, Britta Love, David Khalili, Rachel Robbins, Shanna Butler, Anna Howland, Joanna Steinhardt, Sami Fink, and H. Shay.

Thank you Heidi Lypps and Leah Montange for your guidance in helping me to navigate and understand the history and political theory behind chapter 12.

To the many, many people who have taken the time to educate me about the oppressive impacts of the white supremacist capitalist patriarchy that I have been ignorant about: thank you. I could not have written this book without you.

To my friends who have heard endless hours of emotions about this book on masked walks and video calls during the COVID-19 pandemic: thank you for listening. Each of you has buoyed my spirit through the bleakest of times. Special thanks to Liam O'Donoghue, Elizabeth Sy, Kelly Lou Densmore, Dario Martinez, and Elena Gardella.

To my therapist: you know I *definitely* could not have written this book without you. Thank you for your honesty, love, and commitment to my growth.

To my mother: thank you for doing the work to heal with me and for loving me so deeply. Your support is everything to me.

Thank you to my familiar and little teacher, Queen. Your comforts and total rejection of capitalist values inspire me.

And finally, thank you to the ancestors assisting me in big and little ways on this path.

Index

About the Author

LAURA MAE NORTHRUP, MFT, is a practicing psychotherapist and educator in Oakland, California. She is the creator and host of the podcast *Inside Eyes,* a series that explores the use of entheogens and psychedelics to heal sexual trauma. Her work focuses on defining sexual violence through a spiritual and politicized lens, mentoring healing practitioners in creating a meaningful path, and supporting the spiritual integrity of our collective humanity. You can find more information about Laura and her various projects at www.lauramaenorthrup.com.

About North Atlantic Books

North Atlantic Books (NAB) is a 501(c)(3) nonprofit publisher committed to a bold exploration of the relationships between mind, body, spirit, culture, and nature. Founded in 1974, NAB aims to nurture a holistic view of the arts, sciences, humanities, and healing. To make a donation or to learn more about our books, authors, events, and newsletter, please visit www.northatlanticbooks.com.